Revitalizing America's Cities

SUNY Series on Urban Public Policy
edited by Mark Schneider and Richard Rich

Revitalizing America's Cities

Neighborhood Reinvestment and Displacement

BY Michael H. Schill
and Richard P. Nathan
with the assistance of
Harrichand Persaud

WITHDRAWN

Princeton Urban and Regional Research Center
Woodrow Wilson School of Public and International Affairs
Princeton University

State University of New York Press
Albany

Published by
State University of New York Press, Albany

For information, address State University of New York Press, State University Plaza, Albany, N.Y. 12246

Library of Congress Cataloging in Publication Data

Schill, Michael H.
  Revitalizing America's Cities

  (SUNY series on urban public policy)
  Includes index.
    1. Community development—United States—Case studies. 2. Neighborhood—United States—Case studies. 3. Urban renewal—United States—Case studies. 4. Urban policy—United States—Case studies. I. Nathan, Richard P. II. Persaud, Harrichand. III. Title. IV. Series.
HN90.C6S352   1983   307'.3362'0973   83-396
ISBN 0-87395-742-3
ISBN 0-87395-743-1 (pbk.)

10 9 8 7 6 5 4 3 2

To
Betty and Sidney Nathan
Ruth and Simon Schill

Contents

List of Figures, Maps, and Tables

Acknowledgments

The Princeton Urban and Regional Research Center has a strong and continuing interest in what is happening to American cities—both cities as a whole and individual neighborhoods. The study reported on in this volume fits into the second of these two categories. It is an examination at the neighborhood level of the effects on people of neighborhood reinvestment, what the British call "gentrification." The study began four years ago. The initial plan was to conduct a pilot study on the displacement effects of neighborhood reinvestment, using newly available data, in a test neighborhood in Cincinnati, Ohio. Michael H. Schill carried out the plan as the research project for his Princeton University senior thesis. This work proved to be so promising that we decided, with the support of grants from the Ford, Kettering, and Rockefeller Brothers foundations, to undertake a larger study in nine neighborhoods of five cities, using the research design developed in the pilot study. Mr. Schill served as a research assistant at the Princeton Urban and Regional Research Center during the period when this research was carried out. In September 1981 he left the fertile field of urban research for the quieter life of legal studies at Yale Law School, where he is now in his third year.

Mr. Schill and I would like to acknowledge the valuable assistance of a number of people who contributed to this study. William Apgar, Jr., of Harvard University, Bernie Jones of the University of Colorado at Denver, Helen Habbert of Quest Research Inc., David Knowles of Seattle University, and Peter Roggemann formerly of Virginia Commonwealth University served as field associates. Their help, both in the collection and analysis of the displacement survey data, was vital to the success of this study. Special thanks are extended to a large number of student assistants in each city who helped to locate and interview over five hundred persons. We also gratefully acknowledge the assistance of many neighborhood organizers, public officials, academic experts, and real estate agents in the five cities, who were so generous with their time and expertise. The assistance provided by Richard Hanel, of R. L. Polk & Company, was vital to the success of the study.

Several people assisted us in the design of the displacement survey and the analysis of its results. Among them are Carla Cohen, formerly of the U.S. Department of Housing and Urban Development; Robert F. Cook, on the research staff of Princeton University; George Mailath, a Ph.D student in economics at Princeton; Rolf Goetze, formerly of the Boston Redevelopment Authority; George and Eunice Grier of the Grier Partnership; Franklin James of the University of Colorado at Denver; Howard Sumka of the U.S. Department of Housing and Urban Development; Julian Wolpert of Princeton University; and several careful and very interested anonymous readers for the SUNY Press. Several students at Princeton University contributed research assistance to the central staff for this study: David Hardison, Faye Landes, and Jonathan Reingold. Harrichand Persaud, a recent Princeton graduate, deserves special recognition for conducting statistical and econometric analysis for chapter 5.

We would like to thank Lori Davison, Nan Nash, Michele Pollak, and Kathy Shillaber for readying the manuscript for publication. Ms. Davison helped to supervise the displacement survey. David Aiken and Mary Capouya provided valuable editorial assistance.

Richard P. Nathan, Director
Princeton Urban and Regional Research Center

CHAPTER 1

The Setting for Urban Neighborhood Reinvestment

This book describes a study on a subject of increasing importance to persons interested in cities and urban policy—the causes and consequences of neighborhood reinvestment. This phenomenon is known by many names: reinvestment, rebirth, renaissance, revival, revitalization, or resettlement. For the most part, we use the term "neighborhood reinvestment" in this book. The focus of our research is on the costs in human terms of neighborhood reinvestment. Specifically, our study is about the displacement issue—the effects of neighborhood reinvestment on the people who formerly lived in reviving urban residential areas. We focus on neighborhoods where reinvestment has resulted in population shifts—the *inmovement* of better-off residents and the *outmovement* of lower-income residents. This process is often described by the British term "gentrification."

The upgrading of urban neighborhoods also occurs in situations involving the rehabilitation of the housing stock by a population in place. Upgrading by long-term residents has occurred in some of the neighborhoods we have studied. However, since our research interest is displacement, we concentrate on neighborhoods where reinvestment is manifest in population shifts.

Displacement has been the most intense and controversial political issue surrounding neighborhood reinvestment, both nationally and locally. What is its magnitude? Are the people who are displaced made worse off as a result? The process of reinvestment is discussed in chapter 2; the displacement issue is examined in chapter 3.

There has been considerable debate and yet relatively little research on displacement as a consequence of neighborhood reinvestment, probably because the subject is an extremely difficult one to study.

Once households leave a neighborhood, it is often difficult or impossible to locate them. This is especially true after one year, when forwarding addresses are no longer available from the post office. Locating outmovers is also difficult when they do not have a telephone or when they leave the city or region. Even when outmovers are found, they may be unwilling to provide information to researchers. If this were not enough, there are also likely to be difficulties in getting accurate information, even from cooperative outmovers, assuming one has an adequate sample of such persons.

The Research

These are the problems we have tackled in this research. A pilot study to locate and interview outmovers from a neighborhood experiencing reinvestment in Cincinnati, Ohio, was conducted in 1979. Because this effort was successful, in 1980 and 1981 we undertook a larger survey in nine neighborhoods in five cities. The group that conducted the research consisted of a central staff and academic researchers in each of the five cities. Altogether, 507 interviews were conducted by mail or telephone or in person. This response was from a sample of 1,439 persons, resulting in a response rate of 35 percent. A detailed discussion of the methodology of this study and descriptions of the neighborhoods examined appear in chapter 4.

The five cities chosen for study were selected for both research and practical reasons. They are older cities, experiencing neighborhood reinvestment on a substantial scale, for which recent back-to-back annual address registers on a neighborhood basis were obtainable. These lists enabled us to identify outmovers—persons who resided in the study neighborhoods in year one (1979), but were not listed as residents at the same address the next year. The aim of the interview was to ascertain which households were displaced as a result of the inmigration of higher-income families and whether those households were worse off as a result. Two reinvestment neighborhoods were selected in each of four cities—Boston, Cincinnati, Richmond, and Seattle—and one in Denver.

This survey of outmovers to assess the displacement effects of neighborhood reinvestment is the largest we know of. The neighborhoods we studied are, in demographers' terms, customized. That is, they were identified as reinvestment neighborhoods and defined in terms of census blocks, using information from interviews, direct observation, and local data. The study areas vary in population from

Richmond's Oregon Hill with 843 persons to a portion of the North End of Boston, with 3,592 persons.

Specifically, we studied the following neighborhoods:

- Boston: The North End is an Italian neighborhood on the waterfront, and the South End was predominately blue collar prior to gentrification. Both are adjacent to the city's central business district.
- Cincinnati: Corryville, which is less than two miles from downtown, lies between the University of Cincinnati, a federal office building complex, and a medical center. Mulberry-Vine-Sycamore, an area of old stone houses, is located on a hill with an attractive view. Both had populations that were heavily black and low-income before gentrification.
- Denver: Baker, an area close to downtown, was a relatively high-income neighborhood when first developed around the turn of the century. As the Victorian houses deteriorated, the neighborhood became predominantly low-income, with a large Hispanic population. Reinvestment is taking place with the help of improvements funded by the federal and city governments.
- Richmond: Jackson Ward, the city's historic black quarter, and Oregon Hill, a small area that was primarily blue-collar and white, are both close to the city's central business district. One area of Jackson Ward contains many large brick houses that had been allowed to deteriorate; Oregon Hill is made up of more modest homes, many of which have been kept in good repair.
- Seattle: Mann-Minor, a predominantly black area, was one of the city's most blighted neighborhoods in the sixties and seventies. North Beacon Hill, an area of lower-middle-class households, has experienced an influx of Chinese, Japanese, black, and Indochinese families.

The results of the displacement survey summarized in this chapter and presented in much greater detail in chapter 5 are subject to several caveats. Neighborhoods were chosen according to several criteria, which included a requirement that the area be primarily residential. Although an effort was made to select neighborhoods and cities representative of areas throughout the country where reinvestment is occurring, the unique locational, historical, and demographic makeup of every community presents a major challenge for statistical analysis. The decision to interview outmovers from specific neighborhoods rather than to select a citywide random sample has both pluses and minuses. It made the study more efficient and more manageable, and yielded a much higher number of displaced respondents than would have been possible with a citywide survey. At the same time, it made the application of statistical tests more difficult and uncertain.

Moreover, we recognize that the most transient households are likely to be underrepresented in the sample, since they are less likely to be detected by the door-to-door canvasses relied upon to construct a listing of outmovers. Although the response rate of 35 percent is the highest achieved to date by anyone using this type of research method, if the households that were not located and interviewed differ greatly from those that were reached, the data could be biased. We have relied upon experts to minimize and come to terms, as best we can, with these kinds of problems. As a result, we are convinced on the basis of the statistical tests we have conducted and reported that the effect of bias is not great enough to alter the study's major substantive conclusions.[1]

The Policy Context

All of the cities studied are older cities where previously deteriorated neighborhoods had become candidates for reinvestment. We need to ask in this introductory chapter: What has happened to these older cities that makes it important now for urban scholars to examine the reinvestment process? The answer to this question gets us into a large subject area. The conditions of the nation's older cities have changed. Not only have they changed in population size and population mix, but their role in the economy and the society has changed. Many have lost manufacturing industry and jobs and have become service centers. In the process, some of these older cities with particularly high levels of distress have become the repositories of a growing urban underclass—low-skilled or unskilled persons, who are unemployed or irregularly employed, who have little or no education, and who are often dependent on welfare.

The impact of government programs established over the past forty years to deal with these kinds of urban problems is, to say the very least, hard to assess. Would cities be worse off had there been no urban programs? This question may be impossible to answer definitively. We do not have a comparison group of old, declining cities in which nothing was done—no urban renewal, no welfare, no social services, no public housing, no job and training projects. Perhaps we could compare cities in which there has been little public spending with those in which there has been a great deal. But, here too, as is often true for social scientists, the task of analysis is made difficult by differences in ethnicity, race, region, economics, and the roles of various types of governments and governmental institutions.

Scientific analysis aside, the current mood of the country is one of negativism about the efficacy of public programs to relieve urban problems. There is growing consensus that the nation should rely more on the private sector to save the cities—if they are to be saved at all. Federal and state programs to encourage private investments in older cities are enjoying increased popularity. This has been particularly true over the last five years. From the enactment in 1977 of President Carter's urban development action grant (UDAG) program to Ronald Reagan's proposal to establish "urban enterprise zones," the idea that government can "leverage" private resources with subsidies to private firms is at the center of what serious discussion there has been recently about urban policy initiatives.

This desire to rely more heavily on the private sector has another aspect that is important for our study. Some people have suggested that the best way to aid declining cities and deteriorated neighborhoods is to let them alone, to let private market forces reclaim land and buildings that have fallen on hard times. Proponents of this view cite evidence that, with little or no government intervention, reinvestment has occurred or is occurring in many neighborhoods in older, deteriorating cities. Our study of the displacement effects of urban residential reinvestment sheds new light on this subject from the point of view of the households and individuals affected by neighborhood upgrading.

Urban Conditions

The issue whether older, distressed cities are benefiting materially from private development also raises the broad policy question whether the relative position of cities in which reinvestment is occurring has improved. The last few years have seen a major shift in the rhetoric surrounding public discussion of the prospects for older cities. In contrast with the earlier prevailing wisdom, which had defined the older city as an obsolete economic life form, many recent reports on urban conditions have been much more optimistic. Some observers have argued that decreases in family size and increases in energy and housing costs make central cities more attractive places to live

5

compared with suburbs; they point to neighborhood reinvestment and downtown development in many cities as evidence of urban revival.

In spite of these optimistic reports and in spite of physical evidence like the reconstruction of Baltimore's Inner Harbor and Chicago's North Shore, a doubling of median office rents in Manhattan in the last five years, and impressive amounts of housing rehabilitation in such areas as Adams-Morgan in Washington and Prospect Hill in Cincinnati, it is far from clear that older large cities, as a group or in substantial numbers, have turned the corner. The evidence available to date provides little cause for optimism about the future of the nation's distressed cities.

During the 1970s, people, jobs, and wealth continued to move out of older cities into newer, more prosperous ones. By almost any reasonable measure of the prosperity of places—levels of population, income, employment, economic activity, and concentration of low-income households—the more distressed cities were relatively worse off in the late seventies than they had been a decade earlier, compared to newer and more prosperous cities, which were found to be appreciably better off.[2] The evidence that is available does not support the idea that the urban crisis is over or that it has moderated to an appreciable degree. More detailed studies using data from the 1980 census survey of one out of six households may show a change in this picture, but these data were not available for analysis at the time the study reported in this volume was completed.

An important but often overlooked point for urban analysis is that each city is unique. Some central cities are sprawling jurisdictions that resemble suburbs rather than the more prototypical compact, densely developed city. Regional differences alone do not account for these kinds of variations. Not all northeastern and midwestern cities are old, isolated, and declining. The population of Columbus, Ohio, grew by 44 percent from 1950 to 1970 and continued to grow—though at a slower rate (4.6 percent)—in the seventies. Atlanta, Georgia, on the other hand, grew rapidly in the fifties and sixties (by 49 percent), yet *declined* by 14.1 percent in population size in the seventies. According to census data, all of the cities we studied lost population in the last decade. The big losers were Cincinnati, which lost 15 percent of its population between 1970 and 1980, and Boston, which lost 12 percent.

Results and Policy Implications

Our findings about the amount and consequences of displacement show that, although the amount of displacement occurring in the nine neighborhoods was high, it did not appear to cause significant hardship among those forced to move. Overall, 23 percent of those who moved from the neighborhoods in 1979–80 did so because of displacement. Of those displaced, however, only 16 percent indicated that their current home was worse than the one they had lived in before they were displaced. Sixty-seven percent of the displaced households reported that their housing actually improved. When asked to compare their old and their current neighborhoods, 56 percent of the displaced households rated the new neighborhoods as better than the old. Housing costs rose for displaced households, but at a lower rate than for households that moved for reasons other than displacement. Similarly, the median number of persons per room remained constant for displaced households.

The statistical analysis in chapter 5, employing a probit model, indicates that whether or not a household was displaced had little to do with whether that household felt that its housing situation had deteriorated. Instead, other variables—such as an increase in crowding, the number of times the household had moved in the past ten years, whether it was headed by someone who was unemployed, and the marital status of the household head—better explained whether or not the household experienced hardship. Among the displaced, only two characteristics seemed to predict whether a household would be worse off in terms of housing—whether its head was unemployed and whether it had moved more than five times in the preceding ten years. These findings showing that displacement does not lead to a decline in housing or neighborhood satisfaction, increased crowding, or rapidly rising housing costs are supported by most empirical studies on the subject, although they have been based, as noted, on much smaller samples and response rates.

In chapter 6 we conclude that, at the time the study was completed, the advantages of neighborhood reinvestment outweighed its disadvantages, at least those disadvantages resulting from displacement. Neighborhood reinvestment involving the influx of higher-income households to urban neighborhoods should be encouraged by federal and local policy. Whenever possible, localities should attempt to minimize displacement and, in those instances where it is unavoidable, assist in relocation. The best way for cities to protect against displacement becoming a problem as reinvestment progresses is for them to take steps to remove barriers to mobility and increase low-income housing opportunities.

CHAPTER 2

Neighborhood Revitalization

Although the revitalization of once-declining neighborhoods has occurred occasionally in the past, the scope and frequency of reinvestment seem to have grown considerably in recent years. A body of literature is just beginning to form that seeks to answer many questions about the revitalization process. How much reinvestment is currently taking place in American cities? What forces have led to this increased interest in inner-city housing on the part of higher-income households? Which neighborhoods are the most likely to be revitalized and how does this reinvestment proceed? How might neighborhood revitalization benefit the residents of the inner city? This chapter discusses these topics by analyzing the existing literature on reinvestment and presenting new data on the benefits of revitalization.

The Magnitude of Reinvestment

Evidence is abundant that neighborhood reinvestment is occurring in many cities. Although researchers have suggested plausible explanations for the movement, they have not been able to make reliable estimates of how many middle- and upper-income people are participating in it. The phenomenon is too recent, and reliable methods of gathering data are difficult to devise.

The lack of firm data has not stopped some writers from describing the reinvestment movement in superlative terms. Richard E. Reed's comments illustrate this hyperbole: "The so-called urban preservation movement seems to be the most dynamic grass-roots, populist expression by the American people since the great westward agrarian movement of the late 1800s."[1] Enthusiastic articles in the popular press, like T. D. Allman's "The Urban Crisis Leaves Town,"[2] have, however, provoked sharp responses that, to the contrary, urban decline continues apace.

A recent study by the Princeton Urban and Regional Research Center shows that, even though many older cities have pockets of revitalization, they still suffer from economic decline, decay of housing, and fiscal distress. The authors note that for most large cities there are no current data that would allow researchers to determine whether a city's condition has changed in recent years.[3] Research by John L. Goodman, Jr., shows that, on the whole, American cities lost population during the first half of the seventies, while suburban areas enjoyed increases. Goodman concludes that the flight to the suburbs has not yet abated, because more than two-thirds of the loss in central-city population was caused by people who moved to the suburbs.[4]

To dispel the image of a "revived" central city, the Department of Housing and Urban Development (HUD) issued a working paper in 1979, demonstrating that cities were still losing jobs and people and that most cities were falling further behind suburbs in median income and jumping ahead in unemployment rates and proportions of residents below the poverty level.[5] The HUD paper included Census Bureau findings that from 1975 to 1977 the average income of families moving out of the central city was $1,000 higher than the income of those who moved into urban areas, indicating that cities continued to lose higher-income households. For the most part, however, using city-suburban population and income differentials does not appear to be a satisfactory way to assess neighborhood reinvestment. Although many people refer to neighborhood revitalization as a "back-to-the-city" movement, in reality most people who move into reviving neighborhoods come from within city boundaries. All empirical studies completed to date of households moving into these inner-city neighborhoods indicate that Dennis Gale's characterization of neighborhood reinvestment as a "stay-in-the-city" movement is probably more appropriate.[6]

Like much research on the question of neighborhood change, attempts to determine how much reinvestment has taken place have run into roadblocks. Researchers lack uniform local data on housing rehabilitation. Moreover, the most complete source of data on areas within cities is the decennial census, which quickly becomes outdated.

In 1977, Thomas Black of the Urban Land Institute tried to overcome these obstacles by asking local planners and realtors in all communities with populations of more than fifty thousand to estimate how much private housing renovation was occurring in deteriorating neighborhoods. Black found that in 1977 almost half (48 percent) of these cities experienced some revitalization. This figure jumped to 73 percent when only large cities (those with populations above five hundred thousand) were considered. Black estimates that between 1968 and 1977, about 55,000 housing units underwent rehabilitation financed by the private market. Although this number is small, he asserts that it is increasing rapidly.[7]

Franklin James's 1977 study of neighborhood revitalization also concluded that reinvestment in the central city was taking place on a "broad scale."[8] James analyzed data from the Census Bureau's survey of residential alterations and repairs and found that in 1974 the amount spent for renovations by owners of single-family houses in central cities increased dramatically, even outstripping the amount spent per home in suburban locations. Over the first six years of the seventies, the amount spent on repairs and alterations per home in central cities (measured in 1973 dollars) increased by 39 percent. This increased spending on renovation of central-city homes was matched by a large increase in sweat-equity rehabilitation. James concludes: "Measured by numbers of [maintenance] jobs, central city housing was being nearly as well maintained in 1975–1976 as was suburban housing, a striking change in only 18 months."[9]

In an effort to get an admittedly rough approximation of the extent of inmigration of higher-income households to previously low-income areas, Daphne Spain of the Census Bureau analyzed how often black households were replaced by white, higher-income households. She used data on such shifts, or "successions," as a proxy for data on reinvestment. Spain found that the proportion of housing successions in which blacks were replaced by whites was twice as high between 1973 and 1976 as it was between 1967 and 1971.[10] In addition, Spain found that during the mid-seventies the whites who were moving in had higher incomes and educational levels than the blacks who were moving out. The importance of these findings should not be exaggerated, however. Black-to-white housing turnovers still made up only a small percentage of all central-city successions—2.9 percent in 1973–1976. In most of these transactions, households of one race replaced households of the same race. Moreover, the actual number of shifts in which blacks replaced whites was larger than the number in which whites replaced blacks.

Finally, Conrad Weiler of Temple University analyzed national migratory growth rates and found that between 1973 and 1976 the number of households leaving central cities for the suburbs grew by

6.9 percent, while the number of moves from suburbs to the city increased by more than three times that amount.[11]

Although the available evidence is limited, significant reinvestment has been found in certain cities. According to a recent study by Larry Long and Donald Dahmann of the Census Bureau, differences between median incomes of city and suburban residents narrowed between 1969 and 1975 in such metropolitan areas as Boston, Detroit, Philadelphia, Minneapolis-Saint Paul, and Seattle.[12] In Washington, D.C., considered the nation's leading city in gentrification, officials reported that between mid-1975 and mid-1976 the city's white population grew from 22.5 to 23.9 percent of the total population, the first net increase of whites in twenty-five years.[13]

In sum, at present we know that reinvestment has changed several deteriorated neighborhoods in several cities into fashionable residential areas. We do not know just how much reinvestment has taken place overall, but the most recent data available—which are generally two or three years old—suggest that the phenomenon has not yet affected a large proportion of most cities' neighborhoods.

The overall picture for the near future is unclear. Several observers feel that reinvestment will be limited for several reasons: The economic base of most older cities continues to shrink; a relatively small proportion of the existing housing stock in most cities is suitable for renovation; declining services in many cities will make them unattractive to middle- and upper-income people; and a potential exists for violent confrontations between lower-income current residents and new arrivals with different incomes and life-styles.[14]

These predictions do not, however, take into account many of the causes of reinvestment, such as the trend toward smaller households and the rising cost of suburban housing, which we discuss in the next section. These factors show no signs of disappearing soon. Indeed, James predicts that inflation of land prices and new housing construction costs will continue to make central-city housing prices attractive for the next several years.[15] Moreover, other factors are at work that could cancel out some of the limits to reinvestment. For example, in many older cities the service sector of the economy is growing, generating more white-collar jobs. Existing townhouses are not the only kind of housing that attracts new residents: New townhouses are being built in some cities, and in several places vacant factories and schoolhouses are being converted into apartments. Public services conceivably could improve if economic conditions do, boosting cities' revenues and reducing the fiscal pressures they are now encountering. Finally, public policy can alleviate the problem of displacement caused by reinvestment, perhaps by helping current residents stay in and improve their homes or by helping them find better housing elsewhere. Such efforts could reduce the potential for confrontation.

On the basis of the number of people who said they planned to move in HUD's 1978 survey of the quality of community life, Martin Abravanel and Paul Mancini have predicted that urban population will continue to decline in the near future with no dramatic change in characteristics. However, they believe that the proportion of the city's population who are professionals or consider themselves to be upper middle class will increase slightly, even though absolute numbers of these households will decline.[16]

In summary, neighborhood revitalization is taking place in most large cities, but it appears to be of limited magnitude. In most large central cities, for each neighborhood that attracts reinvestment, there is one or more that undergoes the opposite process—disinvestment. Over the past ten years, however, the extent of neighborhood revitalization has grown, and current demographic, social, and economic forces indicate that this trend will continue at least throughout the decade.

The Causes of Neighborhood Reinvestment

The literature on urban development patterns over the last two decades has provided theories to help us understand why higher-income households leave the urban core and establish residence in suburban locations. Most of these theories suggest that households move outward to consume more space where land values are lower than they would be in the central core. Less affluent households move into the housing these higher-income families leave behind and in turn leave their former housing for even poorer households—and so on down the economic ladder. The current revitalization of inner-city neighborhoods suggests that this trend has slowed and perhaps in some cases reversed itself, as higher-income households return to the urban core. This section explores the reasons such a reversal would occur.

Theories of Spatial Location

The most frequently cited theories of urban spatial patterns are the economic models of R. Muth, William Alonso, and Edwin Mills.[17]

Essentially, these models assume that employment is concentrated in the urban core and that the journey to work constitutes the major transportation cost for most households. In the core of the city, commercial, industrial, and residential users compete for scarce space, so land values are highest closest to the center and decrease with distance from the center. The major analytical tool of these economic models is the "bid rent curve" (see figure 1). According to this concept, a particular household decides how it wants to make the trade-off between relatively cheap land in the suburbs and easy access to downtown in the center city. Most of the economists who use this model predict that higher-income households will locate at the periphery, thereby consuming more space than they could near the

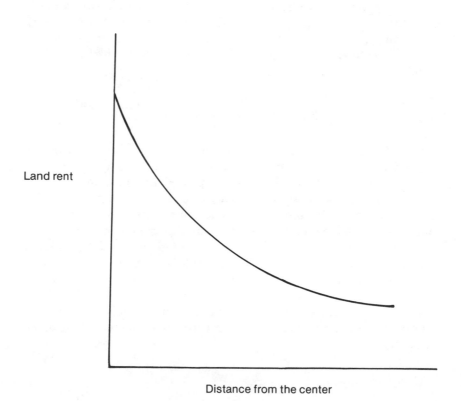

Distance from the center

Figure 1. The Bid Rent Curve

core while spending additional time and money commuting to their jobs in the center. The poor will locate in the center at high densities so as to minimize the costs of land and transportation.

Although these land-use models have most frequently been used to explain the creation of affluent suburbs, they can also explain the location of affluent neighborhoods near the central business district. Economists would say that in such neighborhoods the bid rent curve of the inmovers must be steeper than the curves of both the poor who live in the central city and the inmovers' suburban counterparts. That is, the well-to-do people who move into revitalizing neighborhoods value both land and accessibility, and can afford to pay for them both. They thus outbid all other groups for land close to the urban core. Figure 2 illustrates this bidding for land. Curve *AA* represents a lower-income household's bid rent curve, *BB* represents an upper-income suburban dweller's, and *CC* the inmover's. If *X* denotes the center of the city, the inmigrant will consume land denoted by segment *XD*, the poor household will locate on segment *DF*, and the upper-income suburban household will live on land to the right of point *F*. Before reinvestment, the poor would have consumed segment *XF*. This diagram shows how they have had their location choices narrowed by the influx of upper-income households.

Economic land-use models can tell us that some upper-income households put a high value on homes close to a city's center, but we also need to know why some households are like this and others are not. We also need some way to tell whether or not the factors that lead households to pay steep prices for inner-city homes are likely to grow stronger in the coming years.

Several researchers have done work on these questions. Clifford Kern compared the incomes and household makeup of the people who lived in central Manhattan with those of the inner ring surrounding that core, the suburbanlike outer boroughs of New York City, and those of the city's actual suburbs. He found that high-income households made up of unrelated individuals were particularly likely to live in central Manhattan.

Kern also compared households living in high-income census tracts of central Manhattan with suburban households of similar income levels. His results suggest that the households that were much more likely to live in the central city were of three types:

• Those with only one household member;
• Husband-wife households with no children under eighteen; and
• Those including adults with at least some college.

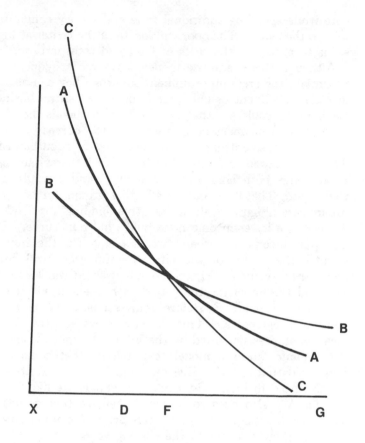

Distance from center

AA lower-income household
BB upper-income suburban dweller
CC inmover to center city

Figure 2. The Bid Rent Curve of Three Households

Kern concludes that distance to work is not the only factor that affects a household's decision about where to live, and that taste plays an important role.[18]

Wendell Bell's sociological theories of land-use choice patterns also attempt to distinguish households that choose to live in the center city from those of similar incomes that live in the suburbs. Bell hypothesizes that households possess one or more of three value

16

systems: "familism," "careerism," or "consumerism." The typical suburbanite adheres to the pattern of familism, which includes early marriage and childbearing and a "high valuation of family living," whereas careerist and consumerist households are most likely to move to inner-city neighborhoods. Those who typify careerism "engage in career-relevant activities to the partial exclusion of alternative activities," whereas those who follow consumerism "eschew both career and family life" and instead prefer "as high a level of living as possible in the present."[19] It is easy to see why the careerist or consumerist would prefer city to suburban life, since the urban core provides the most opportunities for both employment and leisure. In addition, the small size of these households reduces the need for spacious suburban homes.

Demographic Causes of Neighborhood Reinvestment

If the explanations offered by Kern and Bell are accurate, then the recent inmigration of upper-income households to the urban core may be a result of several demographic changes that have occurred in the last decade or two. First among these changes is the rapid increase in the number of households competing for a limited housing stock. As table 1 indicates, the number of households in the United States has grown since 1960 by more than 26 million, an increase of almost 50 percent. From 1970 to 1980 population grew by slightly over 11 percent, while the number of households increased by over 24 percent.[20]

A major reason for the increase in number of households is the coming of age of people born during the post-World War II baby boom. Between 1970 and 1985, the number of people between twenty-five and thirty-five years old—the prime group to form families—will increase by over 14 million; it will then taper off and after 1990 begin to decrease.[21] The swelling of this age group by the baby-boom cohort will mean intense competition for existing housing units, in both the central city and the suburbs.

Social Factors

Another factor leading to the rapid increase in the number of households is the skyrocketing of the divorce rate in the United States.[22] Because divorce means that one household becomes two, this increase in marriage dissolution has swelled the number of households.

17

Table 1 NATIONAL POPULATION AND HOUSEHOLD TRENDS, 1960-1980

CATEGORY	1960	1970	1980	PERCENT CHANGE		
				1960–1970	1970–1980	1960–1980
U.S. population (in thousands)	183,285	203,849	226,505	11.2	11.1	23.6
Households	52,799	63,401	79,080	20.1	24.7	49.8
Nonfamily households	7,895	11,945	20,695	51.3	73.3	162
Single-person households	6,896	10,851	17,861	57.4	64.6	159
Median size of household	3.33	3.14	2.75	-5.7	-12.4	-17.4

Sources: For 1980 data: U.S. Bureau of the Census, *Households and Families, by Type: March 1980 (Advance Report),* Current Population Reports, Population Characteristics, Series P-20, no. 357 (Washington, D.C.: U.S. Government Printing Office, October 1980), and unpublished population data.

For other population data: U.S. Bureau of the Census, *1970 Census of Population: Number of Inhabitants, U.S. Summary,* vol. PCCID-A1 (Washington, D.C.: U.S. Government Printing Office, December 1971).

Another reason for the growth in the number of households since 1960 has been the increased number of households made up of only one person and of households comprising unrelated individuals. Between 1960 and 1980 single-person households jumped from 13 percent of all households to 23 percent, while the percentage of households made up of unrelated persons rose from 15 to 26 percent.[23] One major reason for this increase is that large numbers of young people are moving away from their parents but marrying later.[24] In addition, because women have a higher life expectancy than men, the number of widows living alone has increased. The single-person household is especially likely to bid for housing in the center core, primarily because a single person requires little space.[25] Furthermore, the younger single person is likely to want to be close to leisure activities, and many single elderly persons want to be close to the sources of social services.

This increase in single-person households has combined with a decrease in birth rates[26] to cause a decline in the size of the average American household, which in turn implies a greater demand for smaller housing units. These are most often located in cities. Table 1 shows that the average household size decreased from 3.33 in 1960 to 3.14 in 1970 and to 2.75 in 1980.[27]

An increase in the proportion of women in the labor force over the past two decades might also fuel reinvestment in cities. In 1960 only 38 percent of all women over the age of sixteen held jobs, but by 1980 this percentage had jumped to 52.[28] In households where the wife works, the couple may decide not to have children at all or to postpone reproduction and, as mentioned earlier, childless couples tend to have fewer reasons for avoiding city life. An increase in female workers could also mean two household members working in the central city, which might tip the balance against locating in the suburbs, far from work. Finally, the increase in female participation in the labor market may account for women being able to afford to leave their parents' households and live alone. These single-person households have been one of the principal sources of demand for older homes or apartments in reviving neighborhoods.

Thus the major demographic and social trends of the past two decades—the increase in the number of households and the decrease in average household size—both fit into the theoretical framework developed by Kern and Bell to predict revitalization of central cities. An increase in the number of single-person households and childless couples should result in heightened demand for central locations. The apparent movement away from the life pattern of "familism" should also strengthen the chances that a household will live in the city and not the suburbs.

Changes in Urban and Suburban Housing Markets

Acting in concert with the demographic and social trends outlined above, changes in urban and suburban housing markets over the past decade have fueled the process of neighborhood reinvestment. One factor leading to an increase in the value of both urban and suburban housing stock is a long-time trend toward homeownership. Since 1950 the proportion of American households who own their own homes has risen from 55 to 65 percent.[29] Townhouses in the central city that had been subdivided into apartments have been purchased and transformed into single-family, owner-occupied dwellings. One reason the demand for homeownership was strong during the 1970s is that housing served as a hedge against inflation. According to a recent report by the Robert A. McNeil Corporation, the median price of a single-family house increased from $18,000 in 1963 to over $62,000 in 1979.[30] During the seventies the value of housing went up faster than the consumer price index, making investment in housing lucrative. The McNeil Corporation estimates that from 1968 to 1979 investment in single-family housing had an annual compounded rate of return of 9.6 percent, while other conventional investments such as stocks returned only 3.1 percent per annum.

Federal tax policies have worked hand in hand with inflation in the housing market to increase the desirability of homeownership and thereby fuel reinvestment in central-city neighborhoods. The tax laws are currently biased in favor of homeownership, leading many households to "overconsume" housing.[31] For example, the government does not tax the housing services or imputed rent an owner derives from his home. In addition, homeowners are entitled to deductions for mortgage interest, property taxes, and some types of renovation expenses. None of these tax benefits is available to those who rent.

Many households that desire the advantages of owning their own home have discovered that they cannot afford a single-family house. Developers have met the demand by converting older apartment buildings in the city—including many deteriorated buildings—to condominiums. Such conversion has in many inner-city neighborhoods been the primary vehicle for reinvestment (see table 2).[32]

The condominium combines many of the advantages of ownership with those of renting. Condominium owners receive the tax advantages of homeowners and can also take advantage of the appreciating value of their property. The condominium, however, is usually cheaper per square foot than the single-family home. In addition, condominiums often meet the limited size requirements of small households more closely than detached houses. Finally, condominium owners do not have to do much of the maintenance required of the single-family homeowner, usually paying a monthly maintenance fee instead.

According to Franklin James, the relatively low production of new housing since 1974 has driven up the prices of new homes, and

Table 2 ANNUAL CONDOMINIUM CONVERSIONS, 1970–1979

	1970–1975	1976	1977	1978	3 QUARTERS OF 1979	TOTAL
Total U.S. condominium conversions	82,540	19,452	43,546	74,462	108,370	328,370
Percentage of nation's rental stock converted	0.32	0.08	0.17	0.30	0.43	1.31

Source: U.S. Department of Housing and Urban Development, *The Conversion of Rental Housing to Condominiums and Cooperatives* (Washington, D.C.: U.S. Government Printing Office, 1980), page IV-6.

thereby greatly increased the desirability of inner-city homes relative to those in the suburbs.

In recent years, new housing has increasingly become a luxury reserved for relatively affluent families. Many housing consumers, faced with a choice between modest, basic new homes and older homes available in the existing stock have decided that older housing is the better buy.[33]

Greater reliance on existing housing increases the desirability of central-city homes, which are often less expensive than existing suburban housing. Various studies have shown that currently the median value of suburban owner-occupied units is between one-quarter and one-third higher than the value of similar housing in the central city.[34] Among the causes of rapidly increasing suburban housing values are the escalating cost of new construction, rising land prices, and the spread of growth restrictions in many suburban jurisdictions. As Bernard Frieden states, recent developments in the housing market tend to favor urban reinvestment: "For the first time in the postwar period, housing economics is working in favor of this return [to the city]. The high cost of suburban homes, both new and existing, makes the price of older in-city housing a bargain by comparison."[35]

Changes in Urban Employment Bases

Changes in many cities' economic bases also contribute to revitalization. Since the fifties, central cities have lost much of their industrial and manufacturing employment base because factories and warehouses have fled to suburban and exurban locations. On the other hand, while manufacturing jobs in central cities have fallen, over the past two decades employment in service sectors has grown.[36] Perhaps the most dramatic growth in central-city service employment has occurred in corporate and financial offices. According to Thomas Black of the Urban Land Institute, corporate and bank executives "continue to value central locations because of the benefits of face-to-face contact among the professionals and managers and the economies in the agglomeration of different high-grade and specialized service and other business and financial activities."[37] To illustrate this dramatic increase, Black reports that the average increase in office space in the core areas of twenty large U.S. cities from 1970 to 1978 was 43 percent.[38] Other sectors of the urban service economy that have increased significantly over the past decade include speciality retailing centers, such as Boston's Quincy Market and Baltimore's Harborplace, and government services.

The transformation of the cities' employment base from one requiring lower-skilled industrial workers to one requiring more educated and skilled service workers has fueled reinvestment in inner-city neighborhoods. An influx of employees to central locations often translates into a heightened interest in living nearby. Lipton's study of residential location in the twenty largest American cities shows that, indeed, those cities that have white-collar central business districts and significant commuting distances between suburb and core were the most likely to contain higher-income neighborhoods near the center.[39] Not only are centrally located neighborhoods inherently desirable to those who work nearby, they also often benefit from public and private improvements that spill over from the expanding central business districts, such as street repairs and the opening of retail stores and restaurants.

The Effect of Rising Energy Costs

Since the 1973 oil embargo and the subsequent rise in energy prices, many observers have predicted, perhaps wishfully, that high energy prices will lure households back to the city or at least change the minds of those who were planning to move to the suburbs.[40] High gasoline prices, of course, increase commuting costs, and as economic land-use models indicate, higher commuting costs should increase the slope of an individual's bid rent curve, leading him or her to economize on transportation costs by moving in toward the central city. Despite the intuitive appeal of the argument, many urban analysts have criticized these predictions as simplistic. A study conducted by Bruce-Briggs indicates that instead of moving into the city, suburban households will economize by switching to higher-mileage cars: "The notion that higher gasoline prices will seriously hinder mobility and put an end to suburbanization is probably wishful thinking by those with an animus toward suburbia."[41] In addition, a recent simulation by Kenneth Small of a "worst possible case" of gasoline prices rising to $1.67 per gallon in 1977 dollars leads to a similar conclusion. Small estimates that the most a suburban family working in the city could save by moving to the city would be about $123 per year, a sum he notes is small when compared to most families' total incomes and housing costs. He concludes that he can find "little support for the view that overall urban decentralization

22

will be substantially altered in the next one or two decades by energy shortages."[42]

The Role of the Public Sector

In addition to their role in providing tax incentives for home-ownership, governments often influence reinvestment directly or indirectly through urban policies and subsidy programs. Although the federal urban renewal and model cities programs typically did little in the short run to attract middle- and upper-income households, some areas that are experiencing today what appears to be private reinvestment did receive funds from those programs in the past. Examples are Philadelphia's Queen Village, which received urban renewal funds, and Cincinnati's Mount Auburn neighborhood, which received money under the model cities program. Some analysts have speculated that the current community development block grant and urban development action grant programs might encourage reinvestment by providing subsidies for renovation or simply by making city neighborhoods more attractive through site improvements.[43] Data on this point are not yet clear. Phillip Clay found that as of 1979 only one-fourth of the 105 revitalized neighborhoods he studied had used community development money,[44] but both of these programs are relatively new, and their effects may take several years to become evident.

Some government actions to increase the availability of mortgages in central-city neighborhoods may be encouraging reinvestment. The Federal National Mortgage Association has begun to reorient mortgage lending toward investment in middle-income housing in the central city.[45] Also, provisions of the Community Reinvestment Act of 1978 require mortgage lending institutions to disclose where they made their loans, thus presumably discouraging them from "redlining," or refusing to make mortgage loans in inner-city neighborhoods. So far, however, little empirical evidence is available on what effects these developments have had.

Local initiatives can also spur neighborhood revitalization. For example, in New York, legislators and community organizers have criticized the city's J-51 tax rebate program for fueling investment in already overheated neighborhoods. Under the J-51 program, owners who rehabilitate their property receive two tax advantages. Taxes on the value of the improvements are forgiven for twelve years, and the owner receives an abatement of taxes on the unimproved property value for up to 50 percent of the costs of rehabilitation.

23

A Trend toward Historic Preservation

Another important spur to reinvestment in inner-city neighborhoods is the burgeoning interest in historic preservation. Many of the buildings currently being renovated by higher-income households in previously declining neighborhoods are more than a century old. In many cases entire revitalizing neighborhoods have been declared historic districts, entitling owners to several federal and local tax benefits (discussed later in this chapter). Some examples of these revitalizing historic districts are Columbus's German Village, Cincinnati's Prospect Hill, Alexandria's Old Town, and Brooklyn's Park Slope.

The current upsurge of interest in renovating older buildings mirrors the increased sensitivity to and interest in their past shown by many Americans. In recent years, the number of organizations dedicated to historical preservation has risen dramatically. For example, in 1965 only a hundred cities had commissions dedicated to the protection and preservation of historic landmarks and districts. By 1980 there were six hundred such cities.[46] Some observers have tried to explain this sudden interest in the past by suggesting that in the face of a rapidly changing society, many grasp symbols of the past for a sign of permanence.[47] Others argue that the renewed interest in the past results from the "psychological need to re-experience successes of the past because of the disappointments of recent years— Vietnam, Watergate, the energy crisis, pollution, inflation, high interest rates, and the like."[48]

In some instances the desire to renovate older buildings may arise as a backlash reaction to modern architectural styles. Many feel that new buildings are cold and without character, whereas older structures are "more humane in terms of scale, texture, and design."[49] In addition, older buildings may have more tangible advantages, such as sound construction and energy efficiency. Sometimes the impetus to renovate older, often historic buildings comes from external threats to these structures. For example, private developers' plans to alter or demolish these buildings can mobilize citizens to take steps to preserve the properties either by having them declared historic landmarks or by purchasing them. During the fifties and sixties older buildings were frequently threatened by urban renewal clearance projects. Designating an area as a historic district forestalls both the private and the public sector from significantly altering the area by such means as clearance.

The renovation of inner-city historic buildings and communities results as much from economic as from cultural or emotional incentives. Perhaps the most important impetus to historic preservation is the 1976 Tax Reform Act. Under this federal law, owners of buildings certified as historic are entitled to several tax benefits if they renovate their structures. They may either amortize the costs of rehabilitation over five years or accelerate depreciation on the total value of the improvements. The act also allows owners to obtain tax credits for the cost of rehabilitation. A study recently completed by the National Bureau of Standards illustrates how powerful these incentives are in encouraging rehabilitation. A developer who in 1975 undertook new construction would have saved between 4 and 9 percent in taxes compared to one who rehabilitated an existing property. In 1977, however, after passage of the act, an owner of a certified historic building would have saved between 13 and 28 percent by renovating.[50] Cities frequently provide incentives of their own for rehabilitating historic structures in the form of property tax abatements and exemptions.

From the time the 1976 law went into effect until 1979, over 750 structures were rehabilitated and yielded the prescribed tax advantages to their owners; over $424 million was invested in these buildings.[51] A recent survey by the Heritage Conservation and Recreation Service, the agency that used to administer the certification process, indicates that over nine out of ten of its respondents felt that "a greater awareness of the potential for rehabilitation exists in the communities as a result of the tax provisions."[52] Respondents included government planners and historic and preservation commissioners as well as realtors, developers, and owners of certified historic buildings.

Changed Attitudes toward the City

Attitudes toward city life may also be changing. These changes may encourage reinvestment, but their effects are less measurable than those of other factors. For the past thirty years middle- and upper-class people generally saw suburbs as a refuge from the problems of the city, yet recently such problems as crime, juvenile delinquency, and family instability have been on the rise in the suburbs.[53] According to Harvard University's Charles Harr:

People thought of the suburbs as their refuge from the toils of the world, where Norman Rockwell would paint their daily life. But particularly in the last 10 years, the suburbs in the East and Midwest have become the heirs to their cities' problems. They have pollution, high taxes, crime. People thought they would escape all those things in the suburbs. But like the people in Boccaccio's "Decameron," they ran away from the plague and took it with them.[54]

Although a majority of Americans surveyed in 1978 said they preferred to live outside the city,[55] some segments of the middle and upper classes have come to see the advantages of city life. Some who tried the suburbs now see them as too homogeneous and lacking in community spirit.[56] Those who already live in the city presumably see less and less reason to move to the suburbs, and so stay in the city if they look for new housing.

Recent Homebuyers in Revitalizing Neighborhoods

The most widely accepted of the above causes for the apparent increase in revitalization holds that demographic and social trends have interacted with housing market trends to make revitalization a desirable alternative. Larger numbers of relatively young, affluent, and small households have entered the housing market at a time when central-city house prices are relatively low. Several studies completed since 1976 on the characteristics and intentions of households moving to revitalizing neighborhoods seem to confirm this explanation. This section summarizes the findings of surveys of recent home purchasers in revitalizing neighborhoods in Atlanta,[57] Baltimore,[58] the District of Columbia,[59] New Orleans,[60] Philadelphia,[61] and St. Paul.[62] Data from the Census Bureau's 1978 Annual Housing Survey[63] of recent homebuyers in metropolitan areas are used as the baseline for inmovers to all types of neighborhoods. The characteristics of inmovers to the revitalizing neighborhoods are compared with these national survey data to learn whether the inmovers differ in some respects from all movers in metropolitan areas.

For the most part, the characteristics of the households moving to revitalizing neighborhoods seem to substantiate the description of inmovers summarized above. Each of the studies that provided information about the age of the household head found that on the average, recent homebuyers in revitalizing neighborhoods are younger than those in the national sample of all metropolitan homebuyers. In addition, in the studies that report information about the size of the household, the proportion of single-person households moving into revitalizing neighborhoods tended to be significantly larger than the average for all recent homebuyers in metropolitan areas. In terms of the proportion of households with children, however, the results are much less clear. The percentages of inmovers to the revitalizing neighborhoods in Atlanta, Philadelphia, and Washington who had children under eighteen were lower than the national average of 49 percent found by the Annual Housing Survey. Inmovers to revitalizing neighborhoods in New Orleans, however, tended to have children in their households more frequently than the national average.

The theory that households moving into revitalizing neighborhoods are relatively affluent tends to be borne out by empirical evidence. Each of the reinvestment studies indicates that inmovers to revitalizing neighborhoods earn higher incomes than the Annual Housing Survey's recent metropolitan homebuyers. For example, in Washington's Capitol Hill neighborhood, 83 percent of recent homebuyers earned over $25,000, whereas the national survey of metropolitan homebuyers reports that only 35 percent earn more than this amount.

The stereotypical image of the "urban pioneer" as young, frequently living alone, often childless, and relatively affluent is thus upheld by the bulk of empirical evidence gathered to date. Another popular conception, which characterizes neighborhood revitalization as a back-to-the-city movement, fails, however, to be borne out by available data. On the contrary, most urban revitalization is the result of what Gale terms the "stay-in-the-city" movement.[64] All five of the neighborhood reinvestment studies that provide information about the location of the recent homebuyer's previous residence indicated that a large majority of these households hail from neighborhoods within the same central city. In fact, only one study shows a larger proportion of households moving into the central city from suburbs or outside the metropolitan area than the Annual Housing Survey's sample of recent homebuyers. According to Franklin James:

> There is little evidence of a back-to-the-city movement. Rather the revitalization of demand for homes in cities is the result of the changing housing needs and changing housing constraints on city residents. This of course does not diminish the importance for cities. It seems reasonable to suspect that many of the young homebuyers now buying city homes would have left the cities for the suburbs under housing market conditions prevailing in the sixties or early seventies.[65]

Another hypothesis, that most inmigrants to revitalizing urban neighborhoods are buying their first homes, does seem to be supported by the data. All five studies show that the large majority (usually two-thirds) of households rented before moving to revitalizing neighborhoods. These proportions exceeded the rates for the typical metropolitan homebuyer, who more frequently owned his own home before moving.

As expected, the affordable price of the inner-city home was consistently mentioned as one of the main reasons why households moving into inner-city neighborhoods bought their current homes. Many also mentioned the investment potential of purchasing these "undervalued" properties. Inmovers frequently mentioned the architectural style of their house and the neighborhood's location as important considerations in their decision to purchase.

The Process of Neighborhood Reinvestment

Neighborhood reinvestment has occurred to some extent in most major American cities. Recent studies have examined the process in such diverse cities as Seattle[66] and San Francisco[67] in the West, Cincinnati[68] and St. Paul[69] in the Midwest, New Orleans[70] in the South, and New York,[71] Philadelphia,[72] and Washington, D. C.,[73] in the East. Those neighborhoods that experience revitalization frequently share several characteristics. In the first place, the majority of neighborhoods are located near the central business district. According to a study of 105 revitalizing neighborhoods by Clay, half of the revitalized neighborhoods studied were located within one mile of the central business district. In addition, most neighborhoods that experience reinvestment share one or more of the following characteristics: high elevation; proximity to water; and the presence of public spaces, parks, and historic landmarks.[74] For example, Philadelphia's Queen Village and Boston's North End are located on or near waterfronts, while Cincinnati's Mount Adams and Seattle's Capitol Hill occupy hillsides overlooking the rest of the city.

Revitalizing neighborhoods often also contain similar types of structures. Most buildings in these neighborhoods date from the nineteenth century. According to Clay, in almost three-quarters of the neighborhoods examined, the majority of buildings were over seventy-five years old.[75] A second property of these dwellings is their low density. Most buildings in communities that have experienced reinvestment are either single-family detached dwellings or townhouses. Finally, the architectural style of these residences is usually distinctive. Clay reports that the most common style of architecture in revitalized neighborhoods is Victorian.[76]

Although the neighborhood reinvestment process often differs in some respects from community to community because of each area's unique historical, physical, and demographic makeup, there seem to be enough similarities to permit construction of a model to describe the phenomenon. The following three-stage model of reinvestment draws heavily upon the work of Clay, Gale, Goetze, the National Urban Coalition, and Pattison.[77]

Stage 1. A few households composed of young, single persons or childless couples purchase and rehabilitate homes in a few blocks of a declining neighborhood. Members of these households are often employed in artistic or design fields. Frequently they consist of homosexual or interracial couples who seek a diverse community in which they will not be subject to the types of social pressures they might encounter in a more homogeneous setting. In addition, they are drawn to these neighborhoods by the availability of cheap, distinctive housing. During this first stage of reinvestment, the inmovers mix well with existing residents, causing little or no tension or disapproval. Goetze estimates that 10 percent of neighborhood newcomers arrive during this stage of reinvestment.

Stage 2. Confidence in the neighborhood as a good investment grows as it is discovered by the news media and realtors. A greater proportion of homes are purchased by investors and resold unrenovated. The public sector often contributes through site improvements or better service delivery. Those households that move to the neighborhood during Stage 2 are still small, but usually composed of more career-oriented persons, such as lawyers and teachers. Households buying homes in the neighborhood during Stage 2 are often attracted by still-reasonable housing prices and the investment potential of their acquisition. Second-stage inmovers frequently do not assimilate into the neighborhood as easily as their predecessors did, running into conflicts with their neighbors over excessive noise and crime. Moreover, tensions rise over the increasing rents and property taxes that result from the increased desirability of the neighborhood. Guilt and the desire for a diverse community often motivate inmovers to try to prevent or limit displacement.

Stage 3. Midway through the last stage of reinvestment, most structures in the neighborhood have been renovated, and very few original tenants remain. The few housing bargains left can be purchased with readily available conventional mortgages. People moving into the neighborhood during this stage are those whom Pattison and Gale term "risk averse." Households composed of an older married couple and children moving in from suburban locations are not uncommon. The head of the household is frequently employed in a professional or managerial position and earns a high salary. More often than inmovers in Stage 1 or 2, these newcomers plan to live in the neighborhood permanently and are thus concerned with preserving values. They frequently organize to oppose zoning variances and subsidized housing and to promote their neighborhood through historic preservation designation. In some communities, Stage 3 inmovers fight with Stage 2 inmovers over such issues as the desirability of diversity and displacement.

Although similar stage models have been proposed by many social scientists, most have not been based on statistical evidence. As part of its analysis of revitalization in twelve neighborhoods, the Research Triangle Institute (RTI) has attempted to evaluate these models by using the extensive data collected on neighborhood change. Although the authors of the study admit that some of the data may imperfectly capture the processes of reinvestment, they conclude that the changes associated with revitalization seldom fit neatly into stages. Instead, the changes occurring in the neighborhoods studied seemed to be "discontinuous and abrupt."[78] For example, increased sales, renovation, and speculation often take place concurrently. In addition, these changes are not continuous. Sales activity and prices in the study neighborhoods did not steadily accelerate but rather rose at first and then leveled off, only to rise again later. Much of this variability can be attributed to macroeconomic forces such as the recession of 1975. In almost every neighborhood that experienced reinvestment before 1974, the process slowed during the recession, then increased dramatically during the economic recovery.

Some evidence reported in the RTI study, however, does support the stage model outlined above. The study finds that in the earlier stages of revitalization more buildings changed from renter occupied to owner occupied than in later years. This confirms the model's assertion that in the earlier stages households bought relatively inexpensive homes. The study also finds suburbanites moving into revitalizing neighborhoods in the later stages, as predicted by the model. Finally, the RTI study finds that in Atlanta's Inman Park, early inmovers tended to perform larger amounts of the renovation themselves than did later inmovers. This finding confirms the model's contention that the early "pioneers" often purchase the building both for its inexpensive price and for the opportunity to rehabilitate using "sweat equity."

It is obvious, then, that because of many neighborhood-specific factors and the economic forces operating beyond neighborhood boundaries, the process of neighborhood revitalization may differ from that predicted by the stage model. For example, reinvestment may spread more slowly in neighborhoods where high proportions of buildings are owner occupied, because owner-occupants have lower mobility and greater security. Neighborhood residents may also attempt to regulate reinvestment. For example, the residents of Philadelphia's Queen Village have used local zoning boards to dampen reinvestment.[79] Thus the speed of revitalization, at least in the earliest stages, may vary inversely with the degree of neighborhood organization. A third factor that affects the process and speed of reinvestment is the availability of mortgage financing. Although most residents of deteriorating neighborhoods have trouble acquiring mortgages and rehabilitation loans from financial institutions, some neighborhoods receive this needed financing with less delay than others.

The foregoing discussion illustrates one of the most important features of neighborhood revitalization—its diversity. Although a stage model is useful in understanding revitalization, it necessarily oversimplifies a complex process. Depending on many conditions, the process may differ from one neighborhood or city to the next. In addition, the causes of reinvestment may also vary greatly, depending on the characteristics and trends of individual areas. In some cities, reinvestment may result from the increased demand of small, affluent households, whereas in others it may be sparked by government intervention.

The Benefits of Neighborhood Reinvestment

In most cities reinvestment did not begin until the mid-1970s. Because many of the supposed benefits of the process require years and perhaps decades to become visible, their true extent remains a matter for conjecture. We can, however, look at several examples of neighborhood reinvestment that occurred in the 1950s and 1960s. Although not similar in all ways to the reinvestment of the 1970s and 1980s, the examples of Baltimore's Bolton Hill, Cincinnati's Mount Adams, Philadelphia's Society Hill, and the Georgetown neighborhood of Washington provide some information about the long-term benefits of neighborhood revitalization. In addition, findings from the Research Triangle Institute's study of the effects of revitalization in more recently changing neighborhoods will be presented where relevant.

Four Mature Revitalized Neighborhoods

Bolton Hill, Baltimore. Once the home of Baltimore's higher-income families, Bolton Hill deteriorated during the 1950s; its median income dropped to 28 percent below the city's median, and its population became disproportionately black. In the early sixties, most of the neighborhood was designated as an urban renewal area, leading to publicly financed clearance and rehabilitation. Privately financed renovators rehabilitated most of the neighborhood's housing stock by the middle of the next decade. From 1960 to 1970 alone, the median income of the neighborhood jumped 136 percent, the proportion of blacks dropped, and the median number of school years completed soared (see table 3).

Mount Adams, Cincinnati. Mount Adams was revitalized as a result of private forces rather than public actions. On one of the city's seven hills, the neighborhood overlooks the downtown areas and had been a stable, working-class community until the mid-1960s.[80] Its location and cheap housing drew higher-income households, and by the mid-1970s, the neighborhood had experienced an almost complete population turnover. The 1970 census captures part of this resurgence, showing rapidly rising property values and increasing incomes.

Society Hill, Philadelphia. Adjacent to Philadelphia's central business district and the Delaware River, Society Hill was developed as the home of the city's "economic and social elite."[81] During the 1940s and the 1950s it declined, but after its designation as an urban renewal site in the early sixties, the decline was reversed. By 1972, about 90 percent of the neighborhood's housing stock had been rehabilitated, and a higher-income population had moved into the neighborhood.[82] House values soared almost 250 percent during the 1960s.

Georgetown, Washington, D. C. Revitalization of Georgetown, a neighborhood located in the western portion of Washington, D. C., was primarily the result of private reinvestment, spurred by a housing shortage that afflicted the District of Columbia in the late 1930s and 1940s. Reinvestment was a slow, steady process that accelerated

32

during the 1950s and 1960s. Since 1940, the proportion of blacks in the neighborhood has plummeted; median income and educational attainment have soared.

Housing Renovation

The most obvious and visible benefit of urban reinvestment is the rehabilitation of a neighborhood's housing stock. As a neighborhood revitalizes, developers or higher-income households themselves renovate dilapidated housing units. In addition, vacant shells are often purchased and renovated for occupancy, thereby returning former fire hazards to the housing stock. Most of this rehabilitation of housing occurs with little or no public expenditure. In each of the four neighborhoods just described, the housing stock was extensively renovated. In Bolton Hill and Georgetown, renovation was assisted by various federal and local programs associated with urban renewal. The revitalization of Mount Adams, however, is most similar to the current wave of reinvestment in American cities, since it was entirely fueled by private sources. According to a study of Phyllis Myers and Gordon Binder of the Conservation Foundation, in just two years, 1970 and 1971, the value of building permits issued for additions, repairs, and alterations in Mount Adams increased from $266,000 to $966,000.[83]

Data collected by the Research Triangle Institute also reflect the extensive renovation that occurs in revitalizing neighborhoods. Of the twelve revitalizing neighborhoods examined, over half have had at least one-third of their properties rehabilitated since the reinvestment process began.[84] Much of this renovation was performed by the owners themselves, with 45 percent of them doing over half of the work. Rehabilitation was not, however, restricted to homes recently purchased by higher-income inmovers. On the contrary, RTI reports that many long-time owners who had not fixed up their homes heretofore began renovating as the neighborhood and their confidence in its future improved. Overall, one-third of the unsold homes in the twelve neighborhoods studied were renovated.[85]

Economic Development

Neighborhood reinvestment often encourages economic development. As higher-income households move into revitalizing neighborhoods, their purchasing power attracts restaurants, stores, and other commercial investments. Tourists drawn to these areas also provide

Table 3 POPULATION AND HOUSING TRENDS IN FOUR MATURE NEIGHBORHOODS

CHARACTERISTIC	BOLTON HILL	BALTIMORE	MT. ADAMS TRACT 12	MT. ADAMS TRACT 13	CIN-CINNATI	SOCIETY HILL	PHILA-DELPHIA	GEORGE-TOWN TRACT 1	GEORGE-TOWN TRACT 2	WASH. D.C.
Percentage nonwhite										
1940	8.2	24.0	18.6	4.0	12.2	10.6	13.0	28.0	13.5	28.2
1950	6.9	26.9	20.1	6.2	15.5	19.4	18.2	17.0	8.0	35.0
1960	47.0	34.7	27.4	2.1	14.2	20.3	26.4	5.0	1.0	53.9
1970	35.4	46.4	9.5	0.4	27.6	6.3	33.6	3.1	1.3	71.1
Median school years completed										
1940	NA	NA	NA	NA	NA	7.5	8.2	11.0	8.7	10.3
1950	10.0	8.6	8.3	8.6	9.0	8.3	9.0	12.9	12.5	12.0
1960	9.7	8.9	8.2	8.8	9.7	9.0	9.6	14.9	15.6	11.7
1970	12.6	10.0	10.4	11.6	11.2	15.3	10.9	16.3	16.6	12.2
Median family income										
1950	2,185	2,817	2,163	2,750	2,644	1,806	2,869	3,869	1,495	2,975
1960	4,096	5,659	4,207	3,504	5,701	4,679	5,782	11,384	9,780	5,993
1970	9,660	8,815	10,259	9,221	8,894	17,825	9,366	21,583	21,335	9,583

Table 3 cont'd

Median house value[a]

1940	NA	NA	NA	NA	NA	4,195	3,362	10,850	7,602	7,568
1950	9,708	7,113	NA	5,815	12,260	5,224	6,990	20,000+	20,000+	14,494
1960	11,200	9,000	6,900	9,400	15,100	13,100	8,700	25,000+	25,000+	15,400
1970	25,100	10,000	10,500	12,220	16,400	45,300	10,600	50,000+	50,000+	21,300

Percentage of housing units owner-occupied

1940	18.3	39.3	11.7	24.1	31.3	17.3	36.9	23.5	24.1	28.1
1950	15.1	50.0	18.9	31.4	37.1	18.5	54.7	26.1	32.6	31.5
1960	10.7	51.7	18.5	31.8	37.8	22.2	58.7	30.4	36.6	26.6
1970	16.9	42.2	11.2	24.7	35.8	21.1	57.0	28.0	38.6	26.6

Percentage of households in same residence as fifteen years ago

1955	31.7	53.7	33.3	52.0	45.3	57.7	59.0	39.4	24.3	39.3

Percentage of households in same residence as five years ago

1965	32.8	55.7	49.9	47.6	47.6	27.0	61.3	33.5	26.5	47.3

Sources:
For 1940 and 1950 data: U.S. Bureau of the Census, *Census of Population: 1950*, vol. III, Series P-D (Washington, D.C.: U.S. Government Printing Office, 1952).
For 1960 data: U.S. Bureau of the Census, *Census of Population and Housing: 1960, Final Reports*, Series PHC (Washington, D.C.: U.S. Government Printing Office, 1961-1962).
For 1970 data: U.S. Bureau of the Census, *Census of Population and Housing: 1971, Final Reports*, Series PHC (Washington, D.C.: U.S. Government Printing Office, 1971-1972).
a. Not adjusted for inflation.

a demand for services and goods. Following the residential revitalization of Society Hill, for example, many stores, cafes, and boutiques opened.[86] Similarly, the commercial sections of Georgetown and Mount Adams flourished after the neighborhoods' revitalization, with restaurants and bars fighting one another for good locations and facilities.

This economic development brings more tax revenue to city coffers; supposedly, it also creates jobs for central-city residents. But at least three caveats must be mentioned. Many of the new businesses, such as those devoted to health and personal care, employ skilled workers, some of whom may live in the suburbs rather than the city. Second, in some neighborhoods new nightclubs and small boutiques with few employees from the neighborhood may replace stores owned and operated by long-time residents, thereby actually reducing employment of neighborhood residents. Finally, commercial development in primarily residential neighborhoods may bring with it congestion and noise.[87]

Less Demand for Public Services

In the view of several observers, neighborhood reinvestment may ease the fiscal problems of many central cities. These observers contend that the new households will provide increased revenue to the city and will not require as many social welfare services as the previous low-income residents. Not all agree with this proposition. From his experience as president of a neighborhood association in Philadelphia's Queen Village, Conrad Weiler asserts that new residents who move in from the suburbs will demand the high quality of environmental services that they had in their old areas. Families with children, he contends, will want improved schools. He also predicts that new residents will request such costly public improvements as cobblestone streets, brick sidewalks, increased parking, and trees.[88]

Weiler's observations are supported by a recent study on the social benefits of historic preservation commissioned by the Advisory Council on Historic Preservation. This study reports that, although reinvestment usually begins as a private venture, city governments often encourage the process by providing "better street lights, trash pickup, and more police protection."[89] On the other hand, Phillip Clay's research on revitalizing neighborhoods concludes, "In general . . . municipal services are not improved, nor are very strong or consistent demands made for improvement in such services, with the possible exceptions of demands by neighborhoods in advanced stages of gentrification and sporadic demands for improved police 'services.'"[90] His observations are supported by Myers and Binder, who report that, for the most part, city officials did not allocate additional resources to support the Mount Adams neighborhood even after revitalization was completed but felt that the neighborhood was capable of "making it" on its own.[91]

Neighborhood Stability

A fourth benefit that reinvestment supposedly confers is increased neighborhood stability. Although amorphous, this concept of stability implies a conviction that the neighborhood is neither declining nor a bad place to live, but rather is a place for families to settle and become part of a lasting community. One would thus expect a revitalizing neighborhood to experience less turnover, and perhaps even an increase in owner-occupancy if it was attracting households committed to remaining in a stable environment. Census data on these indicators for Bolton Hill, Society Hill, Georgetown, and Mount Adams present a mixed picture. The proportion of owner-occupants rose in Bolton Hill and one portion of Georgetown, but fell in Mount Adams, Society Hill, and the other part of Georgetown, showing instead an increase in rental units. Turnover figures, perhaps understandably,[92] also show contradictory trends. The proportion of households living at the same residence for five years or more rose in Bolton Hill, part of Mount Adams, and part of Georgetown. It fell, however in Society Hill and other portions of Georgetown and Mount Adams.

The finding that revitalization may not translate into long-time population stability is understandable intuitively and is also supported by several recent studies of revitalization. Since a large portion of the households moving into these neighborhoods are young and small, one would expect them to be highly mobile. Studies by Gale of households moving into revitalizing neighborhoods in Washington also provide evidence that these inmovers are not necessarily committed to long-term residency. A quarter to a third of the respondents to his surveys indicated that they would probably move within five years, and an even larger portion of respondents were uncertain about future moving plans.[93]

Finally, surveys of inmovers to Philadelphia's Spring Garden and Atlanta's Inman Park also reveal high levels of turnover. A large proportion of the initial inmovers to each neighborhood have moved since revitalization. More than half (57 percent) of the recent homebuyers in Inman Park and 35 percent of those in Spring Garden bought homes from prior inmovers and investors.[94] Moreover, 16 percent of Inman Park residents and 24 percent of Spring Garden residents who had moved to the neighborhood since 1975 have moved more than once within the neighborhood. The authors of the study conclude that "the amount of residential turnover in Inman Park and Spring Garden has not declined as a result of reinvestment."[95]

Certainly, one of the most important indicators of whether a revitalizing neighborhood has become more stable is its crime rate. Many of these neighborhoods were once considered slums, with all of the social pathologies, including high crime rates, usually associated with that type of neighborhood. If revitalization leads to increased neighborhood stability, it should also be accompanied by lower crime rates, an expectation confirmed by the Advisory Council on Historic Preservation's 1979 study of four historic districts. In each of the three historic districts for which data were available, the number of violent crimes as a percentage of citywide violent crime dropped.

> One tangible social benefit of the preservation activity has been a decrease in violent crime. . . . This is attributed to improved living conditions, new and better street lighting, increased residential, tourist, and business pedestrian traffic, and replacement of marginal or vice-related business by legitimate commercial operations.[96]

Data reported by the Cincinnati Department of Police also indicate that crime in Mount Adams decreased even as city crime increased. In 1960, 1.3 percent of all of the city's reported murders, manslaughters, rapes, robberies, assaults, burglaries, larcenies, and auto thefts occurred in Mount Adams. By 1978, this percentage had dropped to 0.4.[97]

Although the amount of crime has dropped in revitalizing neighborhoods as higher-income households move in, it still remains a problem for many. Crimes against property still occur as burglars victimize the new, affluent residents. Interviews with inmovers in two revitalizing neighborhoods in Washington, D.C., indicate that the most serious complaint these new residents have about their new neighborhoods is excessive crime.[98]

Increased Tax Revenue

The benefit most widely proclaimed by city officials and proponents of revitalization is the increase in tax revenue that results from higher

38

property values. The regeneration of neighborhoods allegedly provides needed revenue to fiscally pressed cities with dwindling tax bases. It is not obvious, however, whether these increased values always translate into a proportionate or even a substantial increase in tax revenues. In their argument that the property tax acts to discourage housing rehabilitation in the inner city, some analysts such as Richard Netzer of New York University maintain that "rehabilitation . . . in most cities will result in some increases in assessment."[99] Others such as George Peterson of the Urban Institute argue that to the contrary, "reassessment only infrequently occurs as a result of upgrading and then with a great time lag."[100]

Peterson points to cities such as Baltimore, Philadelphia, and Chicago, which all lack a systematic process for reassessing properties. If reassessment occurs only infrequently, then the increased values attributable to rehabilitation will not be translated into higher tax assessments immediately. Furthermore, according to Peterson, improvements on properties will only be assessed at a fraction of their true value, since cities will try to avoid scaring away potential renovators. Peterson substantiates this contention with the results of a study conducted in ten U.S. cities. Researchers examined 420 parcels, of which 152 had undergone some degree of private rehabilitation. Only 19 were reassessed after four years and then at only a fraction of the value of the improvements.[101]

How much more tax revenue might a city gain from revitalization once the neighborhood's increased property values have been translated into higher property assessments? To get an approximation, we sampled the assessments of properties in Bolton Hill, Georgetown, and Society Hill. Representative portions of each neighborhood were selected, and tax assessments in each study area were collected for two or three points in time—1940, 1960, and 1980.[102] The change in aggregate tax assessments for each neighborhood was then compared with the change in assessments for the entire city (see table 4).

While assessments in the city of Baltimore rose by 31 percent during the twenty-year period from 1959 to 1979, those in Bolton Hill rose by 175 percent, over five times the city rate. A large portion of the increase in Bolton Hill's assessment can no doubt be attributed to sharp reassessments in 1975 and 1978. According to the state assessment supervisor for the city, "some redeveloping city neighborhoods will be hard hit. . . . Increases could range as high as 40 percent or more in some of the city's more affluent neighborhoods such as . . . Bolton Hill."[103]

Table 4 CHANGES IN TAX ASSESSMENTS IN THREE NEIGHBORHOODS

AREA	ASSESSMENT[a] (millions of dollars)			PERCENTAGE INCREASE	
	1940	1960	1980	1940–1960	1960–1980
Bolton Hill[b]	—	6.1	16.8	—	175
Baltimore[b]	—	1,923.8	2,521.0	—	31
Society Hill	13.5	13.4	38.2	-1	185
Philadelphia	3,219.8	5,106.6	8,264.7	59	62
Georgetown	4.6	11.1	110.4	141	895
Washington, D.C.	2,055.9	3,964.0	25,216.1	93	536

Sources: Baltimore: state assessor; Philadelphia: city assessor; Washington: *Lusk Real Estate Directory.*
a. Not adjusted for inflation.
b. Uses assessments from 1959 and 1979.

Increases in Society Hill and Georgetown were of equal or greater magnitude. Over the past two decades the assessed valuations of the properties sampled in Society Hill rose 185 percent, triple the citywide rate. In Georgetown, assessments rose ninefold, keeping far ahead of even Washington's hefty assessment rise. Reports of rapidly increasing assessments, even in fairly recently revitalizing neighborhoods, are sometimes encountered as cities evidently do take advantage of a wider tax base.[104]

Unfortunately we have no data on the rise in actual market value of homes in these neighborhoods, so it is impossible to provide an accurate picture of whether increased assessments are proportionate to increased values. Most of the admittedly unsystematic evidence on this question suggests that, in fact, increasing tax assessments reflect only a part of rising property values. For example, census data show that from 1960 to 1970 alone home values increased by 246 percent in Society Hill, while from 1960 to 1980 assessments increased by just 185 percent. Tax officials admit that even the recent large reassessments in Bolton Hill have not kept up with rapidly increasing market values. A one-to-one correspondence between increased market values and assessments cannot occur, in part because of a ceiling on the amount taxes can increase in one year. In Baltimore, this ceiling is set at 15 percent. Many other cities offer various exemptions and abatements. Some, like New York, exempt the value of improvements from the computation of tax assessments for several years.

Because of the short period that had elapsed between reinvestment and their study, the Research Triangle Institute understandably found that, although tax assessments increased in revitalizing neighborhoods, the amount of the increase was frequently not significantly greater than inflation in assessments in other, nonrevitalizing communities.[105] In addition, the Institute found that increases in assessments do not keep pace with rising property values. The study concludes, "This suggests that the cities are not benefiting as much as they might from the [re]investment in the neighborhoods."[106]

Costs of Neighborhood Reinvestment

The benefits that neighborhoods derive from reinvestment are frequently accompanied by costs. The remainder of this chapter discusses three of these costs: property speculation, neighborhood tension, and a decrease in a city's low-cost housing stock. The remaining cost of reinvestment—the displacement of lower-income residents by rising rents, increasing property taxes, or eviction—is treated in chapter 3.

Property Speculation

Many critics of neighborhood reinvestment contend that one of its costs is the property speculation that often occurs. In the early stages of reinvestment, real estate developers often buy depreciated buildings, vacant or occupied, for nominal prices. As demand for housing in the neighborhood increases, the developers evict existing tenants and sell the homes to inmovers, frequently with little or no renovation. Speculation has come under criticism for three primary reasons: the practices used to acquire homes from previous owner-occupants, the inflation in housing prices that results from the process, and the blockbusting effect of frequent transactions.

Many long-time owner-occupants fall prey to property speculators because, unlike the speculators, they do not know the real value of their property. When offered seemingly generous sums by the real estate developer, owners may sell for a fraction of true market value, and then be surprised by high housing prices when they look for new accommodations.[107] In addition, an owner who refuses to sell may face harassment by property developers. Richards and Rowe examined the unethical practices of speculators in their article, "Restoring a City":

In a kind of reverse blockbusting, speculators comb neighborhoods on foot and by telephone just ahead of the restoration movement, making attractive cash offers to owners. If the owners refuse to sell, the more persistent speculators call in building inspectors who order expensive repairs on the old and dilapidated homes. Homes are bought and sold the same month, week, and even day for profits of up to 100 percent and more.[108]

Many argue that property speculation in revitalizing neighborhoods leads to inflated housing prices. Speculators are accused of doing little or no renovating of these buildings, yet reselling them for profits often in excess of 100 percent.[109] Critics of the high profits earned by speculators assert that escalating prices fuel displacement, make locating alternative housing more difficult, and threaten to shrink the advantage of central-city housing prices relative to the suburbs.

Despite the joy officials feel for increasing property values, rapid price spirals in a few neighborhoods may be counterproductive to the city. Rapid price and rent spirals set off waves of speculation that exploit present and future housing consumers. The competitive position of the central city versus the suburbs for the middle class could be altered if city housing, with poor public services, costs more than suburban housing. Rapid increases in prices lead to displacement not only of low-income families but eventually of young lower middle class families as well.[110]

In defense of property speculation, the Homer Hoyt Institute, an independent nonprofit real estate research corporation in Washington, D.C., published a paper asserting that speculators, rather than instigating the process, merely reflected existing demand and higher values:

What in fact happens is that the demand for housing of higher quality is driving up prices in locations which are very desirable. Speculation occurs as a way of shifting the gain from one owner to the other. Speculation is the *result* of higher prices, not the cause.[111]

If speculation did, indeed, do nothing to increase the value of a neighborhood, then the institute's statement might be accurate. In reality, however, the practice of buying and selling properties with high frequency, a process called "flipping," may result in a form of "reverse blockbusting."[112] A study published by the District of Columbia City Council indicates that as of 1975 speculators in Washington were holding properties, on the average, for only six months.[113]

Because of the displacement it causes, flipping empties a neighborhood of low-income households and thus increases the value of the community to those inmovers who desire homogeneity. Therefore, speculation may indeed increase the value of housing by driving out low-income families.

Neighborhood Tension

Reinvestment sometimes harms cohesive ethnic communities. As middle-income individuals move into these established neighborhoods, their intrusion may lead to conflicts with long-time residents and a dissolution of neighborhood cohesiveness. Often the first reactions toward a higher-income newcomer are a mixture of approval and apprehension. As time passes, tension, triggered by conflicting lifestyles, increases. Many neighborhoods, especially those bound by ethnic and family ties, develop norms that govern everything from socializing on the front stoop to disciplining "rulebreakers." Newcomers often do not share in these norms. In his study of Queen Village, Paul Levy describes how the new residents' behavior conflicted with prevailing norms. He quotes a resident who yearned for the old days: "Nobody sits out anymore. I would love it fifteen years ago to . . . see people sitting out on their steps . . . crude people, good people. Not educated, nothing like that, but just genuinely good people who would give their arms to you."[114]

As more and more newcomers enter the neighborhood, the fabric of life changes. Corner stores and bars become boutiques and discos. Local residents can no longer afford to live in the neighborhood; they leave behind their friends and relatives. As the "urban village" disintegrates, a state of anomie or breakdown of norms occurs. Roman Cybriwsky describes this process in Fairmount, a neighborhood in Philadelphia. In pre-reinvestment Fairmount, neighborhood residents acted together without police interference to maintain order. Following the inmigration of higher-income households, Fairmount underwent a "breakdown in the neighborhood's internal order," which led neighborhood residents to petition the city for a police crackdown on youth gangs.[115]

Not only has neighborhood cohesion broken down in Fairmount, but tension between long-time residents and newcomers has led to a "competition for territory." Cybriwsky relates that neighborhood residents "despise and fear" the affluent inmovers, and that this antipathy has erupted into violence. On several occasions vandals have attacked the property of inmovers and broken windows, slashed tires, and uprooted shrubbery.[116] Not far away in Spring Garden, a firebombing resulted in over $40,000 worth of damage to a newly renovated house.[117]

Disappearance of Low-Income Housing

One of the major social problems of this nation over the past century or so has been how to house low-income individuals and families adequately. The many policy initiatives, such as the 1949 Housing Act, which promised "a decent home and a suitable living environment for every American family," and subsidy programs have failed to achieve this goal. The 1968 Housing Act set as the nation's housing goal for the next decade the construction or rehabilitation of 26 million housing units, 6 million of them for low- and moderate-income households. Needless to say this goal—assailed by some as not high enough—was never met.[118] In 1977, the Harvard-M.I.T. Joint Center for Urban Studies estimated that there were 16.8 million households with one or more forms of housing deprivation. Most common were households living in substandard housing and those living in standard housing but paying unaffordable rents.[119]

The revitalization of previously low-income neighborhoods by higher-income households may further exacerbate this problem. Historically, this nation has relied upon a filtering-down process to house its poor. New housing on the periphery was primarily built for higher-income households whose previous housing filtered down to those of somewhat lower income. The chain continued, and at the bottom, low-income households were able to upgrade their conditions, even though sometimes only marginally, by moving into housing that had once belonged to moderate-income households. Now, however, with new construction at a standstill and the demand for housing reaching unprecedented levels, the process has, in some instances at least, reversed itself. Housing in some areas is filtering up rather than down as higher-income households purchase and renovate central-city homes. With their main source of upgrading shrinking, low-income households are finding it increasingly difficult to find standard housing that costs a reasonable proportion of their income.[120]

Conclusions

Spurred by an increase in the number of small, relatively affluent households composed of young persons, relatively inexpensive prices for existing inner-city housing, an increase in white-collar employment in central business districts, various public sector programs to improve the city, and changed attitudes about historic preservation and central-city living, many once deteriorated neighborhoods in American cities have become revitalized over the past decade. Although neighborhood reinvestment will not immediately end the "urban crisis," the regeneration of inner-city neighborhoods, on the whole, results in substantial benefits for the city and its residents. The rehabilitation of deteriorated housing conserves an important public resource. Economic development leads to increased tax revenues and more jobs. Greater stability in inner-city neighborhoods, including a reduction in crime, improves the quality of life for residents. Finally, higher property values translate into more tax revenues for fiscally distressed cities, allowing them to continue funding vital public services.

Unfortunately, the benefits of neighborhood reinvestment are accompanied by several costs, including those of property speculation, increased neighborhood tension, and further tightening of the low-cost housing supply. The most controversial and perhaps the most serious of the disadvantages of reinvestment is the displacement of neighborhood residents by higher-income households. In chapter 3 we define displacement, describe the process, and examine its consequences.

CHAPTER 3

Displacement

The most controversial cost of neighborhood reinvestment is the displacement of a neighborhood's residents by higher-income in-movers. In many cities, neighborhood activists have accused local and federal officials of deliberately fostering the process and have urged legislative remedies. Despite the extensive publicity about displacement, little is known about how much of it is occurring and what its consequences are. In this chapter we draw together what information exists to define and illustrate the process and to learn about displacement's consequences.

Defining Displacement

As George and Eunice Grier point out, a universally acceptable definition of the term "displacement" remains elusive. The broad definition that they themselves advocate has been the most widely accepted:

> Displacement occurs when any household is forced to move from its residence by conditions which affect the dwelling or its immediate surroundings and which:
> 1. are beyond the household's reasonable ability to control or prevent;
> 2. occur despite the household's having met all previously-imposed conditions of occupancy; and
> 3. make continued occupancy by that household impossible, hazardous, or unaffordable.[1]

The Griers point to other and narrower definitions of displacement that result in ambiguity, such as the "involuntary movement of the

46

poor that takes place as neighborhoods are upgraded."[2] They criticize this definition for not delimiting its terms, "the poor," "neighbor-hoods," or "upgraded." Other definitions that require households to experience hardships following involuntary movement are criticized as too exclusive.[3]

Although the Griers' criticisms of the narrow definitions of dis-placement are well taken, their own definition, admittedly broad, seems too inclusive for our purposes. Under this definition, displace-ment could result from the same factors that cause disinvestment, such as abandonment and arson. Although reinvestment-related dis-placement may occasionally result from forces that resemble disin-vestment, as when a landlord withholds services to empty a building for speculative purposes, most instances of people forced to leave their homes because of deteriorating conditions do, in fact, result from disinvestment. Therefore, in the interest of restricting our discussion to displacement induced by neighborhood revitalization (hereafter referred to simply as "displacement"), we include a fourth and fifth specification. Displacement:

4. occurs as a result of neighborhood reinvestment or upgrading, through, for example, higher rents, conversion to condominiums, eviction for renovation, or increases in property taxes;
5. results in a neighborhood with tenants or owner-occupants of higher socioeconomic status, as measured by income, educational attainment, or occupation, than before.

The Causes of Displacement

The displacement process differs for homeowners and renters. For owner-occupants, displacement results from two factors. As higher-income people move into deteriorated neighborhoods and rehabilitate the existing housing stock, property values rise. Eventually the city reassesses properties in the area, leading to higher property taxes. Many owner-occupants on fixed or limited incomes cannot carry the new tax burden and often have to sell their homes and leave the neighborhood. Owner-occupants are also affected by an increased strictness in code enforcement. As neighborhood property values increase, city code inspectors may enforce code requirements more stringently. Many occupants cannot afford to rehabilitate their homes and cannot obtain loans, so they are forced to move. Students of displacement disagree about whether a third force at work in revitalizing neighborhoods constitutes a form of displacement of owner-occupants. As home values in these neighborhoods increase, owners are sometimes offered irresistible sums of money for their homes; they sell because the opportunity cost of remaining is too high. We do not, however, consider this displacement since the decision to sell is essentially a voluntary one.

Displacement of tenants is much more widespread than the dislocation of homeowners, primarily because tenants are more vulnerable. As property values increase in the neighborhood, landlords often evict tenants either to hold the building vacant for speculative purposes or to renovate the property for lease to higher-income tenants. In addition, landlords may sell the building to owners who convert it to single-family use, thereby displacing the tenants. Another cause of displacement is the conversion of rental buildings to condominiums. Frequently tenants are offered the opportunity to purchase their units, but even when prices are discounted, they are often beyond the reach of existing residents.

Tenants may also be displaced as a result of rent increases in neighborhoods undergoing revitalization. As the neighborhood becomes more desirable, landlords can demand considerably more rent. Sometimes it is difficult to determine whether the rent increases are attributable to the inflation affecting all sectors of the economy or to the especially tight housing market present in revitalizing neighborhoods; however, in many cases, the effect of revitalization is clear as the rise in rents exceeds the inflation rate. People on fixed or limited incomes often cannot afford these increases and are forced out.

In jurisdictions with rent control provisions, the process of displacement is more subtle, yet equally effective. Landlords will sometimes harass tenants by neglecting needed repairs, refusing to provide adequate services, or indulging in physical or verbal abuse. Tenants who move without a formal eviction notice may still be leaving involuntarily. Fergus Bordewich recounts the experiences of Robert Currie, tenant of a rent-controlled apartment, who was displaced by a landlord who wanted to renovate and raise the rents in his apartment building:

> Soon after the super was fired, Widlanski's workmen knocked the windows out of the vacant apartments and, on purpose, Currie alleges, left the water taps running. Winter came, the pipes froze and burst, and water cascaded into the occupied apartments below. Since then, the eighteen remaining residents, in eight apartments, have intermittently

been without water and have suffered constantly from leaky plumbing. During the last two winters heat and hot water were periodically cut off, and later the boiler caught fire, leaving smoke and a slimy residue in Currie's apartment for days. . . . The tenants have protested to Widlanski and to the city but with little relief. Widlanski, meanwhile, offered the survivors $7,500 apiece to disappear within two weeks.[4]

Another cause of tenant displacement is more attributable to national than to local economic forces. Mortgage rates have risen dramatically, from an average of 7.3 percent in 1979 to an average of 13 percent in 1981.[5] When a new owner buys an apartment building or a landlord attempts to refinance his property, financing costs rise dramatically. These costs are passed along to the tenant in the form of higher rent, and the resulting financial burden may lead to displacement.

The Negative Consequences of Displacement

Much has been said about the extent to which displacement harms those forced to move from revitalizing neighborhoods. Most of this debate has relied upon impressionistic evidence, because no readily generalizable, empirical investigation of displacement exists. This section outlines some of the negative consequences most frequently attributed to displacement, including the racial and economic resegregation of inter-city neighborhoods, the destabilization of nearby residential areas, and the personal costs to households. Most of the limited empirical evidence that does exist is presented at the end of this chapter.

Racial and Economic Resegregation

When predominantly white middle- and upper-income households move into neighborhoods occupied by lower-income, minority families, racial and economic resegregation often occurs. In addition, neighborhoods with mixed social classes and races may suddenly lose their diversity as the rising cost of housing displaces the lower-income residents. Carl Holman, president of the National Urban Coalition, has expressed his concern that many of the gains of the past two decades may be jeopardized by displacement:

49

An economic resegregation is taking place which is creating new islands of urban wealth and severely restricting the housing choices of many long-term urban residents. This phenomenon works against the stated federal goal of encouraging "the reduction of the isolation of income groups within communities."[6]

From the limited data available, we can conclude that new residents of revitalized neighborhoods do appear to earn significantly higher incomes than the people they replace, and that, in most cases, the majority of new residents are white. Census data for Georgetown and Society Hill indicate that in these communities neighborhood reinvestment was a cause of "black removal." From 1940 to 1970, the proportion of black households in one census tract of Georgetown fell from more than 25 percent to only 5 percent, while the proportion of black residents in the District of Columbia was rising from 28 percent to more than 70 percent.[7] Similarly, in Society Hill from 1960 to 1970, the nonwhite population fell from 20 percent to only 7 percent, while the city of Philadelphia experienced an 8 percent increase in nonwhite population.[8]

Ironically, the homogenization of revitalizing neighborhoods occurs despite the wishes of many of the earliest inmovers. Several studies have indicated that the first wave of new residents is drawn to city neighborhoods partly out of a desire to live in heterogeneous neighborhoods.[9] Despite the best efforts of many of these people, their arrival generates market forces that end the community's social diversity.

A potentially more negative consequence than the hardships encountered by displaced minorities and the community's loss of diversity is the polarization that displacement causes between whites and blacks in the society at large. Since the primary beneficiaries of revitalization are white—the landlord, inmover, and real estate agent—and the victims are thought to be disproportionately black, displacement has frequently led to racial and class confrontations, both verbal and physical. Articles like *Ebony*'s "How Whites Are Taking Back Black Neighborhoods" and *The Black Scholar*'s "Urban Displacement: Fruits of a History of Collusion" have become commonplace. Here is an example:

Blacks, Browns and poor Whites are being recycled off the prime land in the central areas of many of the nation's oldest cities. Their strong backs and unlettered minds no longer qualify them to be urban guests.

. . . Current recruitment qualifications for urban dwelling have changed from blue-collar and unskilled to white-collar and computer oriented.[10]

The displacement issue threatens the fragile progress this nation has made in "opening the suburbs" to black residents. Ten years ago the goal of desegregating cities by facilitating black movement to the suburbs was looked upon as progressive; today some see it as part of a plan to force blacks out of urban neighborhoods. The recent demise of HUD's regional mobility program in Philadelphia demonstrates how fears of displacement can be used to thwart an attempt to integrate the suburbs. Under this program, the federal government, under section 8 of the National Housing Act, earmarked a special allotment of rent supplements in suburban areas for inner-city households. Although the city administration eagerly accepted the program, it could not proceed alone, and an unlikely alliance of suburban whites and inner-city blacks formed to oppose the program. Among the reasons given by black housing activists for their opposition were fears that the plan was a "conspiracy" to recycle urban neighborhoods by displacing low-income blacks to suburban locations.[11] Black leaders also were apprehensive that dispersing blacks from the inner city would dilute their political strength.[12]

Destabilization of Adjacent Neighborhoods

Households displaced from neighborhoods undergoing revitalization frequently move to nearby neighborhoods with affordable housing. This inmigration of low-income displacees, if concentrated into one or two neighborhoods, can create problems for the recipient communities. If a community is just barely stable in terms of population change and housing upkeep, the sudden influx of low-income households may reduce owner and investor confidence in the area. The sequence of events following this loss of confidence is known from the 1960s. If owners feel the neighborhood may be in trouble, many will defer maintenance or sell their homes, creating instability as houses deteriorate and population changes. The literature on neighborhood change indicates that disinvestment feeds upon itself, reducing a once-viable community to an area of abandoned homes.

It is still much too early to determine whether the displacement caused in one neighborhood by reinvestment brings about the opposite process in another. If one looks to the past, however, one can find some lessons in the massive population displacements that accompanied the urban renewal program. In many cases, the exodus of people from neighborhoods undergoing public redevelopment resulted in the decay of the neighborhoods into which they moved. Some of the neighborhoods that today are experiencing reinvestment were two decades ago deteriorating for that very reason. One factor that probably mitigates against the type of destabilization that resulted from urban renewal is the more gradual pace of today's reinvestment-induced displacement. For the most part, massive dispersal on the scale of two decades ago is not occurring; thus nearby neighborhoods have more time to absorb the displaced households.

A second factor that may reduce the likelihood that nearby neighborhoods will become destabilized is the spillover effect: The positive aspects of reinvestment frequently spread into adjoining communities. Investors may begin buying and renovating buildings in nearby neighborhoods on the assumption that the forces behind the revitalization are strong enough to reach adjacent areas. The tendency of reinvestment to radiate outward, especially from a community in the later stages of revitalization, may cancel out the destabilizing effects of an influx of low-income households on marginal neighborhoods.

Personal Costs to Displaced Households

Perhaps the most significant cost associated with displacement is the personal hardship for those forced to move. Being forced to leave one's home no doubt leads to psychological and emotional difficulties. These households may be separated from family and friends; they may experience a loss of security and a sense of powerlessness. In a study of displacement caused by the urban renewal program, Mark Fried noted that many displaced persons had deep roots in the renewal neighborhoods, and suffered depression, psychosis, impotence, or rage. "This view of an area as home and the significance of local people and local places are so profoundly at variance with typical middle-class orientations that it is difficult to appreciate the intensity of meaning, the basic sense of identity involved in living in a particular area."[13]

For the elderly, the negative aspects of displacement may become magnified because of their limited incomes, long-term residence, and physical or mental impairment. In testimony before a congressional subcommittee, Kathryn Eager, the seventy-three-year-old chairperson of Washington's Emergency Committee to Save Rental Housing, asserted that the problems of elderly persons evicted by condominium conversion are especially serious:

52

Depression will settle like a black cloak around the tenant in his home and the will to live begins to shrivel and often ends in premature death; suicides are attempted and sometimes successfully. Doctors tell me that they are treating more senior citizens for heart attacks and strokes. They call it condo disease.[14]

A more immediate cost of displacement may be the difficulty displaced households encounter in finding replacement housing and settling into their new homes and neighborhoods. Hardly anything is known about what happens to displaced households after relocation. The media and case-study literature are full of stories depicting— sometimes with lurid detail—the problems of displaced families. These problems range from lengthy searches to overcrowded conditions and unsatisfactory accommodations.[15] But little objective information exists, and none is readily generalizable. The next section summarizes the results of the few empirical investigations of displacement completed to date.

A Survey of Empirical Research on Displacement

Although reliable information on displacement is essential for assessing the extent and consequences of the problem, very little is to be found. This dearth does not result from a lack of interest among social scientists, but rather from the methodological obstacles to the study of displacement. The most important of these obstacles is also the most obvious—the people about whom we wish to learn are no longer all in the same place, but have scattered throughout the metropolitan region. Therefore, in order to learn about the experiences of these displaced households, one must first identify and then locate and interview them. The remainder of this chapter surveys the empirical literature. The two main research approaches are outlined and evaluated, and the results of four studies on displacement are presented and discussed.

Approaches to Studying Displacement

To date social scientists have used two approaches to obtain a sample of displaced households. The first involves taking a random sample of all households in a given area to learn who has moved in some given period and why. The best example of this type is the work of the City of Seattle's Office of Policy Planning. In 1979 that office conducted a stratified, random survey of 1,269 households in the city.[16] Within this sample, 100 households were found to have been displaced. Another study using a random sampling method was Sandra Newman's and Michael Owen's analysis of data from the University of Michigan's Panel Study on Income Dynamics.[17] Their sample included 211 households displaced by both disinvestment and reinvestment. Households participating in the panel study originally had been located by random methods so as to approximate the characteristics of the national population. Finally, a 1975 analysis of Annual Housing Survey data also relied upon a randomly selected sample of over 70,000 households, 360 of whom had been displaced in the previous year.[18]

The advantage of this type of research is that the random selection of households makes it possible to use statistical estimates of error in evaluating the results' significance. The disadvantages include the fact that, since the respondents moved from various locations throughout the city, it is difficult, if not impossible to analyze the relationship between neighborhood conditions and reasons for moving. Although it can be determined that a household was in fact displaced, it would be extremely difficult and costly to get a large enough sample from any one neighborhood or type of neighborhood. This problem is illustrated by the income composition of the displaced populations in the Seattle and the University of Michigan samples. A large portion of these movers had relatively high incomes, indicating that their displacement occurred either as an isolated incident in a stable neighborhood or because of tight market conditions in a prosperous neighborhood.

In addition to this lack of neighborhood-specific data, the three displacement studies have other flaws that limit the generalizability of their findings. The Seattle study examined only households that had moved within city boundaries. This limitation effectively excludes those displaced households that moved to suburban and nonmetropolitan areas. Second, the Seattle researchers failed to present data on critical indicators of housing quality such as crowding. Finally, an inherent weakness of any single-city study is that the unique characteristics of a housing market may limit the extent to which a study of that city's displacees can be used to answer questions about households displaced in other cities.

The Newman and Owen study suffers from its confusing presentation of data and its multiple definitions of displacement. The primary definition of displacement includes households displaced as a result of both reinvestment and disinvestment. Although the authors discuss those displaced by reinvestment separately, they do not present enough data to describe their conditions adequately. Instead they rely on sophisticated econometric analysis, which sometimes obscures their findings.

Second, the sample of 95 persons displaced as a result of reinvestment includes people who moved within an eight-year period (1970 to 1977). This agglomeration of movers from such a long time span mixes together people who were displaced in different years and thus encountered varying housing market conditions. In addition, since most instances of neighborhood revitalization accelerated after the recession of 1974, the sample is weighted toward displacees from a time of less inner-city housing market activity. Finally, no data are presented on the households' own evaluations of their new homes and neighborhoods. Although there is some disagreement on the validity of a household's subjective reactions as an indicator of housing quality, most social scientists do ascribe some weight to these feelings.

The study of displacement using data from the 1975 Annual Housing Survey also has definitional problems. The major flaw of this research rests with the wording of the survey's question on displacement. Although increased rent is a major cause of displacement, it was not included as a possible answer. Because of the way the question is worded, the results tend to underestimate displacement of tenants. The survey also fails to report responses from urban and nonmetropolitan households separately. An estimated 10 percent of the sample lived in nonmetropolitan areas.

The second approach to studying displacement has involved selecting neighborhoods experiencing revitalization, identifying households moving from these neighborhoods during a specified time, and determining where these households had moved in order to interview them. The largest study of this kind to date was conducted by the National Institute for Advanced Studies (NIAS) under a grant from the U.S. Department of Housing and Urban Development (HUD).[19] NIAS traced households that had moved from San Francisco's Hayes Valley since 1975.

The identification, location, and interview approach used by this study overcomes the main disadvantage of the random sampling technique of the Seattle displacement study. One is able to choose the type of neighborhood from which the displaced moved and so guarantee that the type of displacement studied resulted from reinvestment in lower-income neighborhoods. On the other hand, this research approach presents its own difficulties. The first problem involves the kind of source to be used in compiling the list of outmover

55

households. One needs an annual listing of all residents of the city. NIAS's use of listings from the R. L. Polk & Company directories seems the most acceptable method even though these directories occasionally contain errors.

The second methodological problem posed by the Hayes Valley studies concerns nonresponse. Initially all one knows about the out-mover household is its name and former address. To find the household's new location, the researcher assumes the role of detective, searching through telephone books and other available listings. Frequently it is impossible to locate households because they are not listed in the telephone directory and leave no other trace behind them. Although the NIAS researchers were generously funded by HUD, they succeeded in interviewing only 185 households out of a total sample of 1,700, for a response rate of 11 percent. When response rates are this low, the researcher must worry about whether his study's sample is biased toward people who are not characteristic of the entire population of outmovers. The study's credibility is undermined if it can not defend itself against such charges. Among the reasons for NIAS's low response was that it attempted to track outmovers back to 1974. Generally, the more time that has elapsed since a move, the harder it is to find a household. Households may break up and reconstitute themselves, individuals may die, and the sources of information used to find the outmovers may grow stale. Second, because of time and bureaucratic constraints, NIAS tried a rather limited number of sources. Finally, the questionnaire used to interview outmovers took more than an hour to administer, which led a number of households to refuse cooperation.

The Magnitude of Displacement

According to data from the 1975 Annual Housing Survey, approximately 500,000 households, or 3.5 percent of all movers for that year, were displaced by private action in 1975.[20] As discussed above, the Annual Housing Survey's definition of displacement underestimates the aggregate number of people forced to move because it does not include those forced out by prohibitive rent increases. LeGates and Hartman estimate that displacement affects approximately 2.5 million persons a year.[21] Newman and Owen estimate that, from 1970 to 1977 approximately 1 percent of all moves originating in urban areas were precipitated by displacement. Since a large portion of the moves Newman and Owen term displacement result from disinvestment rather than reinvestment, the displacement rate attributable to neighborhood revitalization would be considerably lower.

Seattle's Office of Policy Planning estimates that, from 1973 to 1978, 7 percent of all households in the city moved at least once because of displacement. Finally, NIAS concludes that approximately 25.4 percent of its sample of 185 outmovers from San Francisco's Hayes Valley were displaced over the five-year period of the study.

Overall, the empirical literature on displacement in the United States seems to reach contradictory conclusions. Some estimate that millions are displaced annually, while others conclude the number is more likely to be in the thousands. What most do agree about, however, is that in most cities the number of households displaced is growing, in some places at rapid rates.

The Characteristics of Displaced Households

As with estimates of how much displacement is occurring in American cities, profiles of displaced households from the four studies contradict each other. Three of these studies conclude that nonwhites are somewhat more likely than whites to be displaced. Only the Seattle report indicates that whites have higher displacement rates than nonwhites. The Seattle data again differ from the other studies on the age of heads of displaced households. In Seattle, elderly households have a higher chance of being displaced. In fact, the study concludes, nearly half of all elderly tenants have been displaced from their previous residences. The other two studies that provide information on the age of displaced household heads report that elderly heads of households are not significantly more likely to be displaced than those who are younger.

On the question of income, three of the studies confirm that low-income households are more likely to be displaced than middle-income households. For example, the Annual Housing Survey indicates that the median income of displaced households was 25 percent lower than the sample of all movers in 1975. Surprisingly, however, the NIAS, Michigan, and Seattle studies also found that a relatively large proportion of those displaced earned higher incomes. Newman and Owen conclude:

> non-disinvestment displacement is actually a hybrid classification which, by definition, affects housing units inhabited by families at the higher end of the income continuum (such as those units that are to be converted

57

to cooperatives or condominiums), as well as at the lower ends of the continuum.[22]

Both the NIAS and the University of Michigan studies indicate that the displaced are likely to have completed fewer years of formal education than those who move voluntarily. Moreover, Newman and Owen conclude that those who have lived in the neighborhood for short periods are more likely to be displaced. Finally, NIAS reports that in Hayes Valley female-headed households with children had higher displacement rates than male-headed households or childless, female-headed households.

Changes in Rent and Crowding

Each of the four empirical examinations of displacement concludes that being forced to move does not result in paying substantially higher rents. In Seattle, displaced households paid only a small amount more for rent, and although increases were somewhat higher in Hayes Valley, they were still smaller than those paid by nondisplaced movers. The University of Michigan study also concluded that displacement had no significant effect on housing costs. The Annual Housing Survey reports that, surprisingly, the median gross rents of displaced households actually fell after displacement.

On the question of crowding, however, the evidence is less clear. The Annual Housing Survey results indicate that although displaced households lived in more crowded conditions than nondisplaced movers, crowding did not worsen as a result of displacement. On the other hand, Newman and Owen report that displacement does have a statistically significant effect on increased crowding.

Satisfaction with Home and Neighborhood

The three studies that provide information on movers' subjective reactions to their new homes indicate that most displaced households are satisfied with their new homes. A majority—in Seattle, for example, the figure was 52 percent—rated their new homes better than their previous ones. In the Seattle and Hayes Valley studies, in fact, this preference for the new home turned out to be greater among displaced households than among voluntary movers.

On the whole, displaced households also expressed satisfaction with their new neighborhoods, although they were less enthusiastic about them than they were about their homes. In Seattle, 72 percent said

58

that they liked their new neighborhood either better or the same as their old one, while 28 percent responded that they liked it less. Although the results in Hayes Valley were somewhat more positive than those in Seattle, nondisplaced movers tended to respond that their new neighborhoods were better more frequently than their displaced counterparts did.

Destination of Displaced Households

Two of the four empirical studies of displacement provided information on where displaced households relocate. Of those who moved from San Francisco's Hayes Valley one-quarter remained in the neighborhood, another quarter moved to an adjacent area, and only about 8 percent left the city's boundaries. Newman and Owen also report that the overwhelming majority of those in their sample of displaced households remained within central cities.

Conclusions

Although the data diverge on some points, the available studies generally support the following conclusions:

1. Displacement can arise from any of several causes, including rising property taxes or rents; conversion of rental apartments to condominiums; and, in some cases, cutoffs of services and maintenance.
2. Although estimates of the number of households displaced by reinvestment range from thousands to millions, all studies find that the magnitude of the problem has increased in recent years.
3. Findings from most but not all the previous studies suggest that low-income families are hardest hit by displacement caused by reinvestment, though there is some evidence that significant numbers of higher-income families are affected by condominium conversions and other forms of displacement.
4. Displaced families do not seem to pay significantly higher housing costs in their new homes, though the data from some studies suggest they do live in more crowded conditions than before. Whatever the objective indicators show, however, there is evidence that displaced householders are by and large satisfied with their new living arrangements.

Chapter 4

Methodology and Description of Study Areas

As chapter 3 indicates, there are two approaches to gathering empirical data about displacement and its consequences: (1) taking random surveys of citizens of entire cities or metropolitan areas, and (2) identifying, locating, and interviewing outmovers from selected neighborhoods. To ensure the selection of a sample of displaced households from lower-income neighborhoods at the beginning stages of revitalization, we adopted the latter method. The methodology described in this chapter was initially tested in a 1979 pilot study of displacement in Cincinnati's Mount Auburn.[1]

Neighborhood Selection

Cities for the study were chosen from a universe of all cities with populations over 200,000 for which a listing of all residents was available for both 1979 and 1980. From this set of cities, we chose five that contained at least one residential neighborhood currently experiencing reinvestment. The neighborhood had to be at an early enough stage of change so that potential displacees still lived there in 1979.

To identify which neighborhoods met these specifications, we used several sources of information. Initially, neighborhood planners in each city were asked if neighborhoods that fit our specifications existed in their cities. We followed up leads through conversations with neighborhood organizers and community leaders, local academics and researchers, and real estate agents and bankers. The lead author visited each neighborhood and surveyed neighborhood conditions.

Impressions from these discussions and observations from fieldwork were confirmed whenever possible by consulting sources of data that would indicate neighborhood change, such as records of property transactions, condominium conversions, building permits, and population change. Sometimes these statistical sources would provide information useful in describing neighborhood change. In other instances, neighborhood revitalization had not advanced enough to be reflected in these indicators. As Clay notes in his 1979 antidisplacement handbook, "Statistical indicators are not likely to yield early clues to middle class reinvestment."[2] For those neighborhoods in which statistical indicators failed to measure the process, we relied primarily on interviews and secondary sources.

Nine neighborhoods in five cities were selected for the study. They were the following:

Boston: North End and South End
Cincinnati: Corryville and Mulberry-Vine-Sycamore
Denver: Baker
Richmond: Jackson Ward and Oregon Hill
Seattle: Mann-Minor and North Beacon Hill

The second half of this chapter describes each of these neighborhoods in detail.

Identifying Potential Outmovers

For seven of the nine neighborhoods, outmovers were identified by use of computerized canvass files provided by R. L. Polk & Company of Detroit. The Polk Company publishes annual directories of households in hundreds of American communities. The company sends fieldworkers into each of the city's neighborhoods to canvass all residents. Households that appeared in the 1979 canvass for a particular neighborhood but not in the 1980 one were identified as potential outmovers.

For the two neighborhoods in Boston, we used a different source since Polk had not conducted a 1979 canvass. Each year the city of Boston is required by the state to compile a listing of all residents over the age of eighteen for the purposes of validating voter registration lists. Like those conducted by Polk, the canvasses consist of a door-to-door inventory of residents in all sections of the city. We used these lists in the same way as the Polk lists.

Although they are not produced primarily for use in academic research, the Polk and Boston listings have several advantages over other possible sources of population data. Telephone directories include only those households who own phones and want their number listed, while voter registration records include only those who wish to vote. By contrast, the listings used in this study supposedly include all residents in each city. Unlike Census Bureau enumerations, which are restricted by federal confidentiality requirements, the listings used in this study include names and addresses, making possible the identification of outmovers.

Certain categories of households were excluded from the list of potential movers. We removed owner-occupants from the list for reasons relating to our definition of displacement (see pages 64–65).[3] Households that had moved from subsidized housing were not included, because market forces would not affect their reasons for moving, and movers from halfway houses were excluded for much the same reason. A total of 1,775 potential outmovers were identified through this process (see table 5).

Locating and Interviewing Outmovers

In order to carry out a sustained effort to locate and interview households that had moved from the study neighborhoods, we as-

Table 5 SAMPLE SIZE AND RESPONSE RATES

CITY	ORIGINAL SAMPLE	VALID SAMPLE[a]	COMPLETED INTERVIEWS	PERCENTAGE OF VALID SAMPLE COMPLETED
Boston	400[b]	313	129	41.2
North End			67	
South End			62	
Cincinnati	291	231	97	42.0
Corryville	215	178	74	41.6
Mulberry	76	53	23	43.4
Denver (Baker)	310	255	82	32.2
Richmond	164	137	59	43.1
Oregon Hill	90	79	34	43.0
Jackson Ward	74	58	25	43.1
Seattle	610	503	140	27.8
Mann-Minor	345	283	64	22.6
North Beacon Hill	265	221	76	34.4
Total	1,775	1,439	507	35.2

a. The original sample minus those households that never moved or whose members are deceased.
b. Estimate.

sembled field teams in each city. The teams were headed by researchers, most of whom were associated with a local university, and each team employed from two to eleven interviewers. The first task for the field teams was to try to identify households on the list of potential movers that had not actually moved. Occasionally the Polk and the Boston listings indicated that a household that still lived at a certain address had moved away. In order not to waste scarce time and resources searching for people who had not moved, it was necessary to identify these households and delete them from the list. Two methods proved especially helpful in checking the lists. The first involved checking with the post office to see if forwarding addresses existed. If the Postal Service indicated that a household had not moved, this information was verified by a telephone call or personal visit. The other method involved checking mailboxes. Households whose names still appeared on the mailbox were deleted from the sample. Of 1,775 potential movers, 336 were deleted by the use of these methods.

To find the current residence of the 1,439 outmovers remaining in the sample, the research teams used several methods, frequently in combination. Telephone directories and directory assistance were the best sources and the easiest to use. Other sources that turned up a significant number of leads were voting lists and postal forwarding addresses. Actually, voting lists were used for two purposes. The previous year's voting lists provided detailed information about the outmovers—their full names, ages, spouses' names, and the like. Also, current citywide voting lists that were alphabetized could be used to provide a current address of households for which postal records were no longer available. Although post office forwarding orders expire after one year, they did provide several valid current addresses for the outmovers.

Many other sources were used to gather clues to where the outmover households had relocated. Researchers in Cincinnati and Seattle used school district registers of students to obtain parents' addresses. Membership lists of various neighborhood or civic associations were used in Boston and Denver. Less formal methods were also used. Neighbors and landlords sometimes knew where the households had gone or could provide the name and telephone number of a relative or friend who had that information. Depending upon confidentiality rules of the individual organization or the mood of the person contacted, utility companies, government agencies, and social service organizations often made useful client lists available. An innovative method used in Denver was posting outmovers' names in neighborhood stores, restaurants, and other meeting places along with a sign asking for information.

As soon as a household's current address or telephone number was obtained, the field researchers attempted to contact the head of the household to conduct an interview. A questionnaire containing twenty-nine multiple-choice questions and an accompanying cover letter were sent to heads of households with known addresses (see appendix A). For households of unknown addresses but with known or suspected telephone numbers, the field team attempted a telephone interview with the head of household. If the outmover did not respond to the mail survey and did not have a telephone, interviewers went to the house to conduct an in-person interview. Identical interview forms were used for each type of interview. Once the head of an outmover household completed an interview, he or she was sent a five-dollar check in appreciation.

On the average, each field team spent five months locating and interviewing households that had moved from the nine study areas. As table 5 shows, out of a total sample of 1,439 movers, 507 completed surveys for a response rate of 35 percent. Response rates for neighborhoods ranged from 43 percent for the Mulberry-Vine-Sycamore neighborhood in Cincinnati to 23 percent for Seattle's Mann-Minor.

Defining Displacement and Hardship

Our definition of displacement in chapter 3 includes both households that owned their own homes and those that rented apartments. For the purposes of the five-city survey, however, only outmovers who had previously been renters are included. Homeowners were excluded from the sample for two reasons. First, as discussed in chapter 3, displacement of owner-occupants most often occurs when their property tax rises to the point that they find their current housing unaffordable and therefore must sell their homes. Although this type of displacement certainly takes place in some cities, for most of the cities currently under study it does not. Properties in these cities have, for the most part, not been reassessed systematically in recent years, so displacement caused by increased property taxes does not appear to be a significant problem. Moreover, even if some owners in these cities had been displaced, their situations following the move would probably not be comparable with that of the renters, since they would have received money for their homes.

A household was classified as displaced on the basis of the answers given to question 4: "What is the main reason you moved?" Nineteen possible reasons for moving were included, ranging from the desire to live in a better neighborhood to a need to locate nearer one's place of work. Displacement was determined to have occurred if the respondent chose one of the following reasons for moving:

- Rent increased too much
- Evicted by landlord because house had to be fixed up (includes condominium conversion)
- House was sold by landlord

Because a major objective of the displacement study was to learn about the extent of hardship encountered by displaced households, it was necessary to operationalize the concept of "being worse off." Unfortunately, in the interest of obtaining the outmover households' cooperation in completing the questionnaire, the amount of information requested had to be limited. Among the possible objective hardship variables are an increase in commuting time, the time it took to locate the current place of residence, an increase in rent, and an increase in persons per room. We decided that these indicators would not always be reliable indicators of hardship, since they might reflect household choice or a change in household composition. For example, increased rent may result from the inability to find a comparable home at a similar price, in which case one would say that the household has encountered hardship. On the other hand, the rent increase could also result from a conscious decision to improve the quality or location of the housing unit. Similarly, an increase in the number of persons per room could reflect increased crowding or merely a change in household composition resulting from marriage or birth.

Although these objective indicators of housing hardship will be used occasionally under properly controlled circumstances, the primary indicator of hardship will instead be the household's subjective evaluation of its housing and neighborhood satisfaction. Each household was asked to compare its current house and neighborhood to its previous one and rate the current one as much better, slightly better, the same, slightly worse, or much worse.

Methodological Limitations

Very little literature exists to describe and analyze the type of research design used in our displacement study. As mentioned earlier, our method has advantages and disadvantages. This section discusses some of the problems encountered and whenever possible examines their effect on the study's results.

The Role of Time

Time proved to have an important influence on our ability to locate and interview the outmover households. In the first place, one of the reasons for the comparatively high response rate of 35 percent is that the study—conducted in the spring and summer of 1981— examined very recent movers, those who had changed residence sometime in late 1979 or early 1980. As other studies have shown,[4] it is easier to locate households that have moved recently than households that moved some time ago. As time passes, more households "disappear" either through deaths, changes in living arrangements, or departures from the metropolitan region. Increased time between the original move and the attempt to locate and interview households also reduces or eliminates the usefulness of many sources of leads. Postal Service policy requires the destruction of forwarding address records after one year, and neighbors' memories fade with time. Studying only recent movers involved sacrificing knowledge about how the displacement process changes over time in order to increase the likelihood of locating outmovers. Therefore, the study discusses displacement only in 1979 and 1980.

Time was also important in that those teams that spent the most time searching for households and following up on leads tended to have the highest response rates. As one field associate observed, the process really never ends; new leads constantly appear, and more interviews are always possible.

Type of Neighborhood

In recent years, many American cities have experienced rapid growth in the number of individuals lacking any fixed living accommodation whatsoever. The "homeless" or "shopping bag people" frequently make their homes outdoors in the streets or public parks or inside public buildings. Although the plight of the homeless in New York City has attracted the most public attention,[5] there are many indications that the problem exists in cities throughout the nation.[6]

The recent upsurge in homeless people is attributable to several factors including displacement. In past years, indigent transients have lived in "single-room only" hotels (SROs) at extremely low rents. Typically, the SRO is located close to the center of a city, most often in a commercial or mixed-use area rather than a residential neighborhood. In the past ten years, land values in these commercial areas have increased, sometimes even more rapidly than they have in residential neighborhoods. In response, owners of SROs have converted their buildings into condominiums for higher-income households or from residential to commercial use. This disappearance of low-cost accommodations for low-income transient households has been a major factor in the increase of homelessness.[7]

For the most part, an effort was made in this study to avoid neighborhoods that contained high concentrations of SROs or transient accommodations. One reason for this criterion was our desire to concentrate upon households that moved from residential neighborhoods in response to market pressures caused by an increased demand for residential rather than commercial or industrial land. A secondary reason for avoiding areas with high concentrations of transients was the difficulty in using our research methodology to identify and then locate households who move frequently. Therefore, the results of the survey of outmovers do not describe the rate of displacement among the most transient households or examine the problems faced by the homeless.

Neighborhood Comparability

Although all the neighborhoods in the displacement study were chosen according to the same general criteria, each inevitably differs from the others on some characteristics. The forces acting on any two neighborhoods are never exactly the same, nor are the outcomes. For example, a household displaced from a neighborhood with many vacant buildings will have a different experience than a household forced out of a neighborhood with a tight housing market. The socioeconomic and racial makeups of neighborhoods also differ, affecting both the experience of displaced households and their composition in the aggregate. These differences in neighborhood forces, patterns, and compositions should be taken into account whenever the entire sample of outmovers is aggregated across neighborhood or city lines. In interpreting these data, we shall try to point out significant differences among movers from different neighborhoods.

67

The Accuracy of Polk and Boston Resident Listings

Although the Polk and Boston resident listings are the only comparable sources of data appropriate for constructing a sample of outmovers from revitalizing neighborhoods, their use presents some problems. The Polk Company estimates that it misses from 15 to 20 percent of a city's residents, despite follow-up attempts and quality controls. Whether or not Polk interviews *all* neighborhood residents is not so important as whether those it misses differ from those it interviews, thereby biasing the sample. According to geographer Eric Moore, most city directories "are biased toward the more affluent, stable members of the community and consistently underestimate the total number of inmigrants and outmigrants."[8] Field experience with the Polk and Boston resident listings seems to confirm the view that the most transient segments of the population are not included in either canvass.

Another reason our sample may underrepresent transients stems from the timing of the canvasses. Because outmovers are defined as residents who live at an address one year and are no longer there at the time of the next canvass a year later, transient households moving in after the first canvass and departing before the next would elude detection.

The Problem of Nonresponse

Despite a relatively high response rate for this type of research, a large portion of those who moved away from the nine neighborhoods were not found. If these households differed from the sample of households who were interviewed, the results of the study would be biased. A rough way to find out whether located households differ from unlocated ones would be to compare their characteristics and see whether significant differences exist. Although they are certainly not ideal, data included in the Polk canvass tapes do describe some of the characteristics of the entire sample, such as sex of household head, and household size and composition. A standard "t test" was conducted on each of these indicators to learn whether the sample of outmovers found significantly differed from those not found. As table 6 indicates, in every instance the differences between the two groups are insignificant to the 95 percent confidence level.

Even though the household size and the composition of the households interviewed do not seem to differ from those of the nonrespondents, the sample may still be biased in two ways. First, households

Table 6 Significance of Differences in Characteristics of Responding and Nonresponding Households

Characteristic	Frequency for Nonrespondents	Frequency for Respondents	Absolute Value of T-Statistic[a]
Type of housing unit occupied			
Multifamily	391	182	0.35
Single family	209	92	
Sex of head of household			
Male	466	203	1.14
Female	134	71	
Size of household			
Single person	143	73	0.88
More than one	457	201	
Household composition			
Nuclear[b]	25	19	1.55
Nonnuclear	575	255	

Sources: R. L. Polk & Co. 1979–1980 canvass.
Note: These statistics are based on data from Cincinnati, Denver, Richmond, and Seattle. Data for Boston were not available.
a. This is the absolute value of the standard t-ratios for the hypothesis that for each characteristic the means of both groups were the same. The critical value for a 95 percent confidence level is 1.96. Any value that falls below 1.96 allows us to accept the hypothesis.
b. A "nuclear household" is defined as one composed of husband, wife, and children. A "nonnuclear household" is one with any other composition.

at both ends of the income scale may be undersampled. Because many low- and moderate-income people move in with friends or relatives to economize on rent, it may not be possible to identify and locate them. In addition, some households may not be able to afford telephones and so would not be listed in telephone directories, one of the primary sources of information for the field teams. People at the higher-income levels who have unlisted telephone numbers or who moved out of state were also probably undersampled. A second type of possible bias again involves an underrepresentation of the most transient households. They might not be included in Polk directories in the first place, and their frequent moves would make them harder to locate.

The results of this study indicate that, although the bias against finding low-income households might understate the negative aspects of displacement in the aggregate, this understatement is not large enough to change the substantive findings and conclusions (see appendix B). The bias against finding the most transient outmovers, however, could, to a certain extent, understate displacement and its impact.

69

Problems of Definition

The study's definition of displacement hinges upon the movers' ability to identify their main reason for moving. This reliance on the individual's knowledge about why he or she moved may under- *or* overstate the true dimensions of displacement. There are two problems, whose effects may cancel each other out. First, some movers who said they moved because the rent increased too much could actually have afforded the increased rent. In such a case, the decision to move would be voluntary, although the study would count the person as displaced. Second, movers who said they moved because their previous house was falling apart may not have realized that a landlord's lack of attention to maintenance could be an effort to get rid of tenants and gain an empty building for speculative purposes. In this case, movers would not realize that they had been displaced.

As mentioned above, this study emphasizes the movers' comparison of their current home with their previous home as the major indication of relative hardship. Some people have criticized the use of subjective reaction to the living environment as an index of housing and neighborhood quality, on the ground that people may not be entirely aware of their true feelings toward a home or neighborhood and that these "latent" feelings will not surface during a short interview. In addition, some have asserted that surveying people's attitudes may result in unreliable results as moods change because of external stimuli.[9]

Despite these criticisms, the use of satisfaction as an index of residential quality has grown in recent years. Many planners have adopted "participatory planning," in which they ask residents about their preferences before they draw up plans for a neighborhood. Perhaps the main impetus for paying more attention to subjective criteria is the realization that objective indicators of residential quality do not always reflect the qualities the eventual users of a home or residents of a neighborhood feel are important. According to Angus Campbell of the University of Michigan's Institute for Social Research:

> If we try to explain the population's sense of well-being on the basis of objective circumstances, we will have left unaccounted for most of what we are trying to explain. . . . One's home is not only a dwelling, it is a refuge, a place of privacy, a family gathering place, an object of pride. There is much that is subjective and psychological in the way people see their dwelling place.[10]

Neighborhoods Studied

The remainder of this chapter describes the neighborhoods in Boston, Cincinnati, Denver, Richmond, and Seattle from which the outmovers were selected. Information was gathered from interviews with local planners, real estate agents, and residents as well as from written documentation. Population statistics presented here are from the 1980 census (see table 7); the indicators on household composition were compiled from Polk canvasses and real estate sales histories of each neighborhood.[11]

Boston

Since World War II Boston has changed from a heavy industrial and manufacturing center to a supplier of high-technology research and development and services. Although most of the Boston area's high-technology firms are located on Route 128, to the west of the city, the majority of Boston's service-oriented offices are within the city itself. Between 1968 and 1978, more than 90,000 new office jobs

Table 7 POPULATION OF CITIES AND NEIGHBORHOODS STUDIED

CITY/STUDY AREA	TOTAL			BLACK		
	1970	1980	% CHANGE	1970	1980	% CHANGE
Boston	641,071	562,994	−12.2	104,495	126,229	+20.8
North End	4,522	3,592	−20.6	0	0	0
South End	2,264	2,115	− 6.6	68	127	+86.8
Cincinnati	453,514	385,457	−15.0	125,170	139,467	+ 4.2
Corryville	1,338	824	−38.4	953	637	−33.2
Mulberry	2,697	1,900	−29.6	2,133	1,368	−35.9
Denver	514,678	491,396	− 4.5	46,836	59,262	+ 26.5
Baker	4,314	3,359	−22.1	22	44	+100.0
Richmond	249,332	219,214	−12.1	104,761	112,357	+ 7.3
Jackson Ward	1,384	975	−29.6	1,370	936	−31.7
Oregon Hill	1,290	843	−34.7	142	12	−91.5
Seattle	530,831	493,846	− 7.0	36,689	46,755	+27.4
North Beacon	1,939	1,555	−19.8	250	186	−25.6
Mann-Minor	1,962	2,072	+ 5.6	981	808	−17.6

Sources:
a. U.S. Census, Population for Cities of 100,000 and Over by Rank Order, *1980 Census of Population,* Supplementary Reports PC80-S1-5, Standard Metropolitan Statistical Areas and Standard Consolidated Statistical Areas (Washington, D.C.: U.S. Government Printing Office, 1981).
b. 1970 Census Data Book.
c. Interview with Mary Jane McCoy, Bureau of the Census, August 1981.

were created in Boston, while many manufacturing plants were closing.[12]

This shift in Boston's economy has serious implications for the city's housing market. Many of the skilled workers in the new industries are young,[13] and many are recent graduates of the Boston area's twenty-seven colleges. They generally have higher incomes and smaller households than the area's long-time residents. Largely as a result of this influx of new residents, median household size in Boston decreased from 2.9 to 2.4 persons between 1970 and 1980.[14]

Many of these new residents live within the city itself. Boston's vacancy rate, which dropped from 6.4 percent in 1970 to less than 3.2 percent in 1980,[15] reflects the fact that, despite an overall population loss, the demand for housing in the city has increased. Some of this demand has been absorbed by condominiums, which at present make up 2 percent of Boston's housing stock.[16] Despite a 1980 ordinance requiring landlords to give tenants one year's notice of condominium conversion before they can be evicted, observers expect the trend toward condominium conversion to continue. Many higher-income households have moved to some of the city's oldest neighborhoods, particularly Back Bay and Beacon Hill. These neighborhoods are almost completely revitalized and are quite expensive. The continued investment in major office and medical complexes in the city has led to increased reinvestment within these and nearby neighborhoods.[17] Antidisplacement organizations, first formed when the city underwent extensive urban renewal in the sixties, have been vocal in fighting displacement resulting from reinvestment. Although the extent of the problem has not yet been documented, Boston has received funds from HUD for the development of an antidisplacement strategy.

North End. The North End, located on the northern edge of Boston's waterfront, is Boston's oldest residential neighborhood. By 1650 it had been settled by merchants and artisans. It is the site of the first public school in America, Paul Revere's house, and the Old North Church, where Revere hung the lanterns that warned that the British were coming. The North End has been a home to successive waves of immigrants—first Irish, then Jews, and finally Italians. Since the early 1900s the North End has been Boston's "Little Italy," and until recently 95 percent of its population was of Italian descent.[18]

Almost all of the neighborhood's four- to six-story apartment buildings were built between 1880 and 1920 as cold-water tenement housing.[19] Although the North End's tenements are still in fairly good condition, as of 1970 nearly 40 percent of the neighborhood's 4,139 dwelling units lacked complete plumbing facilities.[20] The streets of the North End are narrow. The overall impression is one of extreme overcrowding.

City officials and journalists often laud the North End as Boston's safest neighborhood, and city crime statistics verify that there is less violence and vandalism in the North End than there is anywhere else in Boston.[21] But the neighborhood does suffer from some of the problems common to many older, urban areas. In 1975 median annual family income in the North End was $8,321, as opposed to $9,133 citywide.[22] The decline of many of Boston's waterfront industries during the past twenty years has exacerbated the North End's economic problems. Moreover, after World War II the North End's population dropped sharply from over 15,000 in 1950 to 10,134 in 1970.[23] Although there are signs that the neighborhood's population has stabilized, this extreme decline in numbers has been of great concern to community leaders.

Between 1968 and 1974 the city spent $2.3 million on the North End, with $1.6 million going to renovate public facilities.[24] Later in the seventies the city earmarked $3.8 million for the North End as part of an overall rehabilitation effort covering the entire waterfront area.[25] The Faneuil Hall-Quincy Market development is the cornerstone of this effort. This historic market area, a few blocks from the North End, has been converted into dozens of shops and restaurants. Funded by private investors outside the city, the market is now a major tourist attraction, and a magnet for young professionals who have moved into newly built high-rise apartments in the area and condominium apartments converted from abandoned warehouses.

There are signs that the housing boom in the Quincy Market area has spilled over into the North End. Since 1975 eighty-three housing units in our study area have been converted to condominiums.[26] Some of these units may have been larger apartments that were broken down into smaller units. Other units occupy what were abandoned warehouses on the waterfront.

As table 8 shows, sales figures for the study area in the northern portion of the North End indicate a strengthening housing market.

Neighborhood leaders have expressed concern over displacement resulting from rising rents, particularly among the neighborhood's large elderly population. Boston's rent control law does not apply to many apartments in the North End. At present both the city government and local community groups are trying to convert apartments and warehouses into low-priced condominiums for the North End's

73

Table 8 HOUSE SALES IN THE NORTH END

YEAR	NUMBER OF SALES	MEDIAN SALES PRICE	MEDIAN SALES PRICE IN 1967 DOLLARS
1973	16	$24,000	$15,464
1976	13	26,000	14,849
1979	38	39,250	18,298

Source: Boston Real Estate Transfer Directory.

elderly residents.[27] It is generally felt that the larger problem of the dilution of the neighborhood's Italian base is less a result of reinvestment than it is part of a larger pattern of assimilation and upward mobility.[28]

South End. The South End was originally settled in the midnineteenth century in a landfill adjacent to Boston's central business district. The neighborhood's initial developers built brick and brownstone rowhouses on "London-style" roadways in the hope of attracting higher-income buyers. Bankers and merchants preferred Back Bay and Beacon Hill, so the South End became home to the city's burgeoning immigrant population. Until World War II, the South End was predominantly a stable working-class neighborhood, although an established middle class has always maintained a presence.[29] The South End's housing stock remained stable over time in terms of both quantity and condition, consisting primarily of tenements, lodging houses, and apartment buildings.[30]

During the 1950s the South End's housing stock began to deteriorate, and a significant number of structures were abandoned. In the early 1960s the Boston Redevelopment Authority (BRA) began a massive urban redevelopment program that demolished one-fifth of the neighborhood's housing stock and displaced 2,000 households.[31]

During the mid-sixties private developers began to invest large sums in areas immediately bordering the South End. The Prudential Center complex of stores, offices, and hotels was built on the neighborhood's northwest border. At the same time the major medical centers near the South End—Massachusetts General, Tufts, Boston University-Boston City Hospital—began to expand vigorously. By the early seventies the area surrounding the South End had undergone considerable office expansion, culminating in the completion of the John Hancock Tower, New England's tallest building.

74

The South End quickly began to feel the combined effects of the city's efforts to revamp the neighborhood and of the enormous private development in nearby neighborhoods. In addition to its convenient location and relative affordability, the South End had other attractions for potential white-collar and professional households. Mortgage subsidies and low-interest mortgages were available for those buying homes in the neighborhood. A major public redevelopment program, which included street improvements, park landscaping, and water and sewer line repair, also attracted inmovers. Moreover, many of the neighborhood's homes were still in good condition and were quite attractive, with high ceilings, dramatic stairways, mahogany woodwork, hardwood floors, and brick walls.[32]

Socioeconomic indicators confirm that the South End experienced a major influx of upper-income inmovers during the sixties and seventies. The study area, which incorporates Union Park, formerly contained many lodging houses. In the past twenty years the proportion of residents who are either white-collar workers or professionals has jumped from 19 percent to 62 percent.[33]

Many housing statistics also indicate that the portion of the South End included in our study area has undergone significant revitalization over the past twenty years. For example, lodging houses have dropped from 69 percent of housing units in 1960 to 16 percent in 1978.[34] In 1960 the entire South End was 7 percent owner-occupied; by 1978, the figure was 28 percent.[35] Median rent in the South End jumped from $46 in 1960 to $180 in 1978.[36] Despite a modest decline in median sales price adjusted for inflation, the South End has experienced a rise in the number of annual house sales over the past decade (see table 9). Although the BRA identifies only forty-two condominium units in the study area as of August 1980,[37] the actual number is probably much higher, because the BRA's narrow definition of a condominium excludes townhouses or the small multifamily units that are typical of the neighborhood.[38]

Table 9 HOUSE SALES IN THE SOUTH END

YEAR	NUMBER OF SALES	MEDIAN SALES PRICE	MEDIAN SALES PRICE IN 1967 DOLLARS
1973	21	$26,500	$17,075
1976	8	35,500	20,274
1979	30	32,350	15,152

Source: Boston Real Estate Transfer Directory.

It is difficult to determine the extent of revitalization in the South End, although experts agree that it has been scattered.[39] Segments of the neighborhood, particularly those closest to the city's office district, have high rents, and their residents have high incomes. These areas appear to be totally renewed. Other sections, however, exhibit considerably less change. In any event, as the South End's revitalization over the past twenty years has generally been exponential, it is fair to assume that the neighborhood will continue to undergo significant revitalization. The building of the $350-million Copley Square Plaza on the South End's northern border should accelerate this trend.

During the early years of urban renewal there was widespread and bitter disagreement over both the extent and the proper treatment of displacement in the South End.[40] Today the South End Project Action Committee (SEPAC), the largest neighborhood organization in the South End, is still concerned over displacement in the area. In conjunction with the city, it is making various attempts to stem displacement and build low-income housing for long-time residents of the neighborhood.[41]

Cincinnati

Like many other older, industrial cities, Cincinnati in recent years has lost population and shifted its economic base. The city's population declined from 453,514 in 1970 to 385,457 in 1980, a 15 percent loss. At the same time the city's black population rose from 125,170 to 130,467, increasing from 27.6 percent of the population in 1970 to 33.8 percent in 1980. Between 1960 and 1970 the city lost almost 4 percent of its jobs.[42] Hardest hit were the retail and wholesale trades and heavy manufacturing. Selected service jobs in finance, real estate, and hotel operation as well as in government actually increased during the late 1960s and the 1970s.[43]

Although the city's average household size has declined steadily over the last decade and now stands at 2.5 persons per household,[44] the overall housing market is not very tight. The vacancy rate for all units in 1981 was 7 percent,[45] although the apartment vacancy rate was 3 percent.[46] Condominium conversion has not been widespread in Cincinnati.

Antidisplacement organizations in Cincinnati have been extremely active and have attracted a great deal of local and national media attention. In 1979 over twenty groups, task forces, and committees were involved in displacement issues.[47] The city has reacted to the organizations by forming a relocation office and a counseling center for displaced households. Cincinnati also recently stepped up its construction of HUD section 8 and section 312 housing. In 1980 the city enacted an antidisplacement ordinance, which covers households displaced by city-funded programs but not those displaced by private reinvestment.[48]

Corryville. The Corryville neighborhood of Cincinnati has gone through several changes during its nearly two-hundred-year history. The neighborhood was first settled in 1798 by William Corry, who later became the first mayor of the town of Cincinnati. Corryville was then settled by German immigrants, and remained predominantly German until after World War II. At that point Corryville began to absorb thousands of people displaced by a major urban renewal project in the city's West End. In the late 1960s and early 1970s, Corryville itself became the site of extensive urban renewal, as the nearby university, hospital, and federal Environmental Protection Agency research center built and expanded facilities, displacing hundreds of families. This phase of urban renewal did, however, have positive effects on Corryville. It facilitated street and park improvements and provided some housing rehabilitation.[49]

Despite the millions of urban renewal dollars poured into Corryville, the neighborhood continued to suffer from many of the problems common to older, urban areas. A 1970 Real Estate Research Corporation report classified Corryville in its "worst" category, using the terms "old, black, falling population, transitional" to describe the neighborhood.[50] A city memo described Corryville in 1979 as a low-income, racially mixed neighborhood.[51] This memo also pointed out that housing deterioration was a problem in the neighborhood and noted the run-down appearance of many streets.

Yet the same memo also noted that there had been recent, widespread private investment in an area of Vine Street called University Village, which had been transformed into a stylish shopping and restaurant area catering to students. The memo also mentioned that private residential rehabilitation was taking place in Corryville, albeit on a small scale.

Corryville's new-found attractions for inmovers are not readily apparent. The neighborhood has no view and no distinguishable topography. Some of its buildings are fairly attractive, but most are plain and architecturally undistinguished. It is likely that the neighborhood's primary attraction lies in its location less than two miles from Cincinnati's central business district and its proximity to academic, medical, and research facilities. It is also thought that in the late seventies Corryville began to absorb some of the overflow housing demand from Clifton, an adjacent neighborhood that underwent extensive revitalization during the second half of the decade.[52]

Most local observers agree that residential reinvestment by individuals in Corryville over the past few years has been slow but steady.[53] A number of conventional indicators show that moderate residential reinvestment, especially by white inmovers, is underway. The study area population was 79 percent black in 1970 and 72 percent in 1980. As table 10 shows, Polk data on the study area follow the patterns expected of a neighborhood undergoing revitalization. Between 1972–1973 and 1979–1980, the percentages of female-headed households with children and of households with three or more children declined significantly. At the same time single-person households rose from 41.8 percent to 61.2 percent of all households. Households with professional or managerial heads rose from 14.5 percent in 1972–1973 to 24.3 percent in 1979–1980.

Between 1976 and 1979 building permits for alterations rose from a value of $28,095 to $48,000, and fees for repair permits rose from $21,700 to $42,965.[54] Bank loans for housing improvement in Corryville doubled between 1976 and 1979,[55] a sign of local lending institutions' confidence in the neighborhood's future. Housing sales data confirm the presence of reinvestment in Corryville, showing increases in the number and average prices of sales (see table 11). Recent developments include the conversion of a large building on Eden Street to condominiums. The rental market in Corryville is strong now, with demand especially high among university students.[56]

There has been little recent concern or debate over displacement in Corryville. Local organizations are instead devoting their efforts to increasing their scope and strength in order to accommodate recent inmovers and improve conditions for long-time residents of the neighborhood.[57]

Mulberry-Vine-Sycamore. The Mulberry-Vine-Sycamore Street neighborhood of Cincinnati is sandwiched between the neighborhoods of Mount Auburn and Over-the-Rhine. Although officially part of Mount Auburn, Mulberry shares many of the characteristics of Over-the-Rhine. Mount Auburn was once an elite neighborhood, but its population dropped sharply and conditions deteriorated. More recently, the Prospect Hill section of Mount Auburn, located immediately east of Mulberry, has undergone extensive revitalization. Over-the-Rhine, to the west, never a high-income area, was once an

Table 10 CHARACTERISTICS OF CORRYVILLE HOUSEHOLDS

	ALL H/HOLDS	OUT-MOVERS	IN-MOVERS	ALL OCC. H/HOLDS
		1972–1973		
Percentage of owner-occupied units	20.3	9.9	7.9	23.9
Percentage of female-headed households with children	12.2	8.0	11.9	14.5
Percentage of households with 3 or more children	29.4	22.5	19.1	30.6
Percentage of single-person households	45.9	56.0	62.1	41.8
Percentage of units with professional or managerial head of households	15.5	18.5	17.6	14.5
(sample size)[a]	(368)	(54)	(34)	(303)
Percentage of retired head of households	17.2	8.8	9.0	18.8
Sample size	1,108	225	177	761
		1975–1976		
Percentage of owner-occupied units	18.2	8.8	4.9	21.7
Percentage of female-headed households with children	11.4	8.3	7.0	12.4
Percentage of households with 3 or more children	24.1	19.7	14.8	25.6
Percentage of single-person households	52.7	61.5	67.2	50.3
Percentage of units with professional or managerial head of households	2.18	23.2	28.6	21.2
(sample size)[a]	(358)	(56)	(56)	(293)
Percentage of retired head of households	13.6	9.6	3.3	15.1
Sample size	1,214	276	244	853
		1978–1979		
Percentage of owner-occupied units	16.8	6.2	1.0	19.3
Percentage of female-headed households with children	7.3	3.7	2.9	8.1
Percentage of households with 3 or more children	15.7	6.7	6.7	17.1
Percentage of single-person households	64.9	78.5	80.9	62.7

Table 10 cont'd

Percentage of units with professional or managerial head of households (sample size)[a]	19.6 (225)	23.7 (38)	43.8 (16)	20.6 (165)
Percentage of retired head of households	11.7	4.8	2.4	11.5
Sample size	1,140	242	209	730

1979–1980

Percentage of owner-occupied units	16.8	7.7	2.6	19.5
Percentage of female-headed households with children	5.9	5.1	0.7	6.5
Percentage of households with 3 or more children	17.0	11.0	9.2	18.6
Percentage of single-person households	63.9	73.6	77.8	61.2
Percentage of units with professional or managerial head of households (sample size)[a]	24.0 (200)	22.7 (22)	6.7 (15)	24.3 (177)
Percentage of retired head of households	5.1	5.5	6.5	18.5
Sample size	988	234	153	677

Source: Computed from canvass files provided by R. L. Polk & Company.
a. Sample sizes for occupation indicator are smaller than for other indicators.

Table 11 HOUSE SALES IN CORRYVILLE

YEAR	NUMBER OF SALES	MEDIAN SALES PRICE	MEDIAN SALES PRICE IN 1967 DOLLARS
1973	0	—	—
1976	7	$14,900	$8,613
1979	12	22,900	9,905

Source: Hamilton County Multiple Listing Service.

attractive middle-class neighborhood. Originally settled by German immigrants between 1840 and 1850, Over-the-Rhine absorbed a large wave of Appalachian migrants after World War II, and by 1956 was a run-down neighborhood with the fastest growing crime rate in Cincinnati. During the 1960s many blacks, displaced by the building of the West End highway, moved to Over-the-Rhine and Mount Auburn.[58]

In recent years, even as sections of Mount Auburn have been revitalized, Over-the-Rhine has suffered from extreme decay and disinvestment. According to the *Cincinnati Enquirer*,[59] a hundred businesses left Over-the-Rhine between 1972 and 1978, and by 1978, 29 percent of all Over-the-Rhine stores were vacant.[60] In 1981 the *Enquirer* reported that almost 40 percent of Over-the-Rhine's housing units were vacant.[61] The economic position of Over-the-Rhine families was extremely bad. The average Over-the-Rhine family income in 1970, at $3,364, was 62 percent lower than the city average, $8,894.[62] In recognition of the neighborhood's condition, the city government granted it $3.5 million in federal community development funds.[63]

Throughout the sixties and seventies Mulberry's condition was similar to Over-the-Rhine's. The neighborhood suffered from decay, disinvestment, and abandonment. Yet during the second half of the seventies, local city planners and speculators began to realize that, for several reasons, Mulberry was a candidate for reinvestment. The neighborhood is on a hill and has a view—two valuable characteristics in Cincinnati. Its old stone architecture, although deteriorated, could be made attractive again in the hands of an imaginative renovator. Most of all, observers thought it inevitable that Mulberry would absorb some of the overflow from adjacent Prospect Hill, whose popularity and housing prices were increasing rapidly.

Many statistical indicators confirm that Mulberry was undergoing a limited resurgence during the late seventies. According to Polk data on our study area (table 12), the composition of the neighborhood's households has changed greatly since 1972–1973. Then 45.5 percent of Mulberry's households had three or more children, but by 1979–1980 the figure was down to 28.0 percent. Over the same period the number of single-person households in the study area rose from 30.7 percent to 54.5 percent. Households with professional or managerial heads increased from 12.0 percent to 23.6 percent between 1972–1973 and 1979–1980. Only one statistical indicator, the percentage of female-headed households with children, has not followed the traditional pattern of revitalization.

There are many indications of renewed interest in Mulberry homes. Mortgages for housing in the area increased in value and number from 1976 to 1979[64] (see table 13). The extremely low median price of housing sales is a sign that shells were being bought for speculation. According to one local real estate expert, many shells have indeed been bought, but because of high interest rates many remain unrehabilitated. This source points to Mulberry's subsidized housing and high crime rate as deterrents to more widespread revitalization.

Table 12 CHARACTERISTICS OF MULBERRY HOUSEHOLDS

	ALL H/HOLDS	OUT-MOVERS	IN-MOVERS	ALL OCC. H/HOLDS
		1972–1973		
Percentage of owner-occupied units	19.9	12.7	0.0	22.4
Percentage of female-headed households with children	12.5	18.7	20.3	16.2
Percentage of households with 3 or more children	48.8	65.5	41.7	45.5
Percentage of single-person households	28.0	18.2	36.1	30.7
Percentage of units with professional or managerial head of households	10.9	0.0	8.3	12.0
(sample size)[a]	(147)	(25)	(12)	(108)
Percentage of retired head of households	19.9	14.5	4.2	19.5
Sample size	562	75	74	277
		1975–1976		
Percentage of owner-occupied units	14.9	2.4	6.8	18.4
Percentage of female-headed households with children	13.2	13.3	16.4	16.4
Percentage of households with 3 or more children	33.9	30.8	26.0	35.2
Percentage of single-person households	44.4	51.2	57.5	43.0
Percentage of units with professional or managerial head of households	18.4	14.3	24.1	19.0
(sample size)[a]	(98)	(14)	(14)	(84)
Percentage of retired head of households	19.8	7.3	6.8	23.2
Sample size	485	113	73	293
		1978–1979		
Percentage of owner-occupied units	17.9	10.8	1.7	20.3
Percentage of female-headed households with children	11.7	15.0	16.9	16.2
Percentage of households with 3 or more children	30.6	37.9	18.6	29.3
Percentage of single-person households	48.5	50.8	67.8	47.7

Table 12 cont'd

Percentage of units with professional or managerial head of households	24.2	11.1	28.6	27.5
(sample size)[a]	(62)	(9)	(7)	(51)
Percentage of retired head of households	19.2	16.9	0.0	20.3
Sample size	497	100	59	222

1979–1980

Percentage of owner-occupied units	22.1	9.9	3.4	26.2
Percentage of female-headed households with children	11.0	8.1	10.5	17.1
Percentage of households with 3 or more children	26.3	18.3	13.1	28.0
Percentage of single-person households	55.7	60.6	68.3	54.5
Percentage of units with professional or managerial head of households	20.6	10.0	0.0	23.6
(sample size)[a]	(68)	(10)	(3)	(55)
Percentage of retired head of households	16.5	21.1	0.9	10.0
Sample size	517	99	77	275

Source: Computed from canvass files provided by R. L. Polk & Company.
a. Sample sizes for occupation indicator are smaller than for other indicators.

Table 13 HOUSE SALES IN MULBERRY

YEAR	NUMBER OF SALES	MEDIAN SALES PRICE	MEDIAN SALES PRICE IN 1967 DOLLARS
1973	0	—	—
1976	2	$16,000	$9,249
1979	9	5,000	2,163

Source: Hamilton County Multiple Listing Service.

Certain areas of Mulberry, however, have already been heavily revitalized. These areas include Dorsey and Goethe streets, which have clearly delineated boundaries and are on cul-de-sacs. The houses there are fairly small and have nice views.[65]

The extent of displacement in Mulberry is not known. A study by James Rubenstein classified Mulberry as a high-displacement area, but the study employed an extremely broad definition of displacement.[66] A local organization, People Against Displacement, has been extremely vocal in opposing displacement in Over-the-Rhine and Mulberry. The organization's activities range from lobbying successfully for a city antidisplacement ordinance and conducting a voter registration drive to presenting a slide show and distributing buttons.

Mount Auburn was recently the subject of an acrimonious debate over its possible designation as a historic district. Opponents of the designation claimed that it would squeeze out low-income homeowners who could not afford the prescribed renovations. The fight received widespread attention when a resident of Over-the-Rhine took employees of a Cincinnati television station hostage and, before killing himself, made a tape stating his grievances. His description of living conditions in Over-the-Rhine and his cry, "You are ignoring these people," led to a delay in the designation ruling.[67] Ultimately, parts of Prospect Hill within Mount Auburn became a historic district, but the status of the rest of the neighborhood, including Mulberry, was not changed.

Denver

The city of Denver is experiencing a severe housing crunch. During the seventies, it became one of the nation's major energy centers, second only to Houston. In that decade thousands of energy-related firms opened in greater Denver, and these firms in turn drew tens of thousands of new residents to the metropolitan area. The population of the city itself rose during the sixties and declined somewhat during the seventies, but the population of the Denver SMSA has increased dramatically over the past twenty years—especially during the last ten. The population of the SMSA jumped from 933,929 in 1960 to 1,227,529 in 1970, and then to 1,643,165 in 1980.[68] A decline in average household size, from 2.7 persons per household in 1970 to 2.2 persons per household in 1980, has exacerbated the pressure on the housing market caused by the influx of newcomers.[69] The vacancy rate, reflecting the increased demand for housing in the city, dropped from 4.5 percent in 1970 to 3.0 percent in 1980.[70]

During the seventies Denver's minority population increased from 27.8 percent of the city's population in 1970 to 39.0 percent in 1980. Slightly more than half of Denver's minority residents are Hispanic.[71] The city has also experienced a major, largely undocumented, influx of illegal aliens. Denver has 6,000 public housing units, whose vacancy rate ranges from 1.5 to 2.7 percent.[72]

Private, individual reinvestment is widespread in Denver, particularly in the downtown area. According to Bernie Jones of the University of Colorado at Denver's Center for Community Design, a "back-to-the-city" movement gained momentum in Denver during the late sixties. This movement grew rapidly when, after the OPEC crisis, Denver became a major energy center. Although most of the employees of Denver's newborn energy industries moved to the suburbs, some opted for the city. By the late seventies, many of the first neighborhoods to revitalize had become so expensive that prospective inmovers turned to different neighborhoods, including Baker.

The problem of displacement has attracted the attention of the city government. Denver's official housing policy states:

> In all of the City's housing and neighborhood preservation activities, there is a risk that people will be dislocated. Since it is the City's purpose to preserve its cultural diversity, City agencies and decision-makers must be conscious of this risk, and act to minimize the disruptive effects of revitalization efforts.[73]

Baker. Like many other neighborhoods that underwent a resurgence in the late seventies, the Baker neighborhood in Denver had once been considered a desirable and prestigious place to live. Later, however, Baker had suffered from many of the problems afflicting America's older inner cities. Originally developed in the 1880s, Baker was one of Denver's earliest sections, and its residential sections were completely developed by 1915. Conveniently located barely a mile from downtown and composed largely of attractive Victorian houses set on tree-lined streets, the neighborhood also enjoys easy access to the city's transportation network as well as a view of both the Denver skyline and the Rocky Mountains. But these attractions have, until recently, been offset by some negative outgrowths of the neighborhood's early development. Little residential investment was made in Baker after the turn of the century, and the neighborhood's old houses were allowed to deteriorate. As a result, Baker has for many years been a home for low-income minorities, particularly Hispanics.[74]

In 1970, 6.1 percent of the neighborhood's population was classified as unemployed (the citywide figure was 4.4 percent), and 26 percent of the neighborhood's households were below the poverty level (9 percent citywide).[75] City officials have often expressed concern over some absentee landlords who convert Baker homes to rental units, as well as over the general physical deterioration of the neighborhood.[76] A 1972 community renewal program declared Baker "blighted," and a 1979 study by the Denver Regional Council of Governments designated Baker an area of economic distress,[77] thereby qualifying it for special funding from the Economic Development Administration (EDA).

In 1978 signs began to appear that middle-income households were moving into Baker, radically altering the neighborhood's profile. Young white couples and singles, attracted by Baker's distinctive homes, affordable prices, and convenient location, were apparently buying their first homes in the neighborhood. Many statistical indicators confirm that Baker was, indeed, undergoing revitalization during the second half of the 1970s. According to Polk data on our study area, in 1976–1977 more than 60 percent of all inmovers were single-person households, as opposed to 16.6 percent of all outmovers. Ony 5.7 percent of all inmoving households in 1979–1980 had retired heads, in contrast to 18.1 percent of all outmoving households. In 1973–1974, 15.8 percent of all occupied Baker households had professional or managerial heads. In 1976–1977, the figure reached 18.4 percent, and by 1980 it had risen to 27.9 percent. In fact, all Polk indexes of change conform to the pattern one expects in a neighborhood experiencing revitalization (see table 14).

Figures on house sales in our study area are perhaps the most dramatic indicators of the area's revitalization. The median sales price more than tripled between 1972 and 1979 (see table 15). In 1972 the highest price paid for a Baker home was $26,000; $65,000 was the highest in 1978. It is noteworthy that "condo fever" has not yet hit Baker. As of June 1980, there was only one condominium building in the entire neighborhood.[78]

As private investment took hold in Baker, both the federal and the city governments began to play a role in the neighborhood's development. Funds channeled to Baker enhanced the neighborhood's attractiveness in the eyes of potential inmovers and improved the quality of life for long-time and newer residents alike.

There has been some concern over displacement in Baker. A city research report classifies Baker as a high-displacement area,[79] and local neighborhood organizations have held meetings to discuss the problem. The city has not yet, however, taken any appreciable steps to combat displacement in Baker.

Richmond

The population of Richmond, Virginia—by far the smallest city in our study—increased from 219,958 in 1960 to 249,332 in 1970.[80]

Table 14 CHARACTERISTICS OF BAKER HOUSEHOLDS

	ALL H/HOLDS	OUT-MOVERS	IN-MOVERS	ALL OCC. H/HOLDS
		1973–1974		
Percentage of owner-occupied units	28.2	10.3	12.8	33.7
Percentage of female-headed households with children	9.6	11.5	11.1	9.6
Percentage of households with 3 or more children	20.3	18.4	20.1	21.0
Percentage of single-person households	43.9	46.8	46.4	43.3
Percentage of units with professional or managerial head of households	16.2	16.2	15.5	15.8
(sample size)	(506)	(74)	(116)	(417)
Percentage of retired head of households	26.4	21.6	15.2	28.1
Sample size	1,682	339	343	1,126
		1976–1977		
Percentage of owner-occupied units	26.9	16.6	11.3	31.2
Percentage of female-headed households with children	11.2	11.2	15.7	12.0
Percentage of households with 3 or more children	16.3	15.2	13.9	17.1
Percentage of single-person households	52.8	16.6	60.3	51.1
Percentage of units with professional or managerial head of households	19.4	20.6	20.0	18.4
(sample size)	(402)	(102)	(75)	(288)
Percentage of retired head of households	23.8	15.5	9.3	27.0
Sample size	1,586	355	345	1,022
		1979–1980		
Percentage of owner-occupied units	26.8	12.6	11.1	33.2
Percentage of female-headed households with children	8.0	6.5	7.8	9.7
Percentage of households with 3 or more children	14.8	11.5	10.2	16.4

87

Table 14 cont'd

Percentage of single-person households	57.1	67.5	64.9	52.1
Percentage of units with professional or managerial head of households	27.7	25.6	30.2	27.9
(sample size)[a]	(329)	(82)	(53)	(240)
Percentage of retired head of households	21.0	18.1	5.7	21.9
Sample size	1,578	381	333	925

Source: Computed from canvass files provided by R. L. Polk & Company.
a. Sample sizes for occupation indicator are smaller than for other indicators.

Table 15 HOUSE SALES IN BAKER

YEAR	NUMBER OF SALES	MEDIAN SALES PRICE	MEDIAN SALES PRICE IN 1967 DOLLARS
1972	48	$11,250	$ 8,654
1973	46	10,500	7,913
1976	50	18,000	10,689
1979	82	39,700	17,795

Source: City and County of Denver, Denver Planning Office.

That increase, however, is usually attributed to the city's annexation of outlying neighborhoods.[81] Between 1970 and 1980 the population decreased by 12 percent from 249,332 to 219,214. The proportion of blacks in the total population grew from 42 percent to 51 percent.

The city's economic base remained stable over the seventies, with some growth in the service sector. Although many of the area's small tobacco firms closed in the past decade, the continued growth of Philip Morris, Richmond's largest private employer, has more than compensated for the loss of those jobs. The largest employment sector is government—city, state, and federal—and this sector, too, has remained stable. The number of service-sector jobs in Richmond has increased substantially, from 37,000 in 1973 to 55,000 in 1979.[82] The city's economy is healthy, if not booming. Richmond's housing market is not particularly tight. The value of one-family homes has been rising between 8 and 12 percent annually, and condominium conversion is proceeding at the slow pace of one or two buildings a year.[83]

Jackson Ward. Jackson Ward was first settled in 1793 by a prosperous freed slave. Settlement continued gradually until by the 1860s

88

Jackson Ward was fairly densely populated. Although the neighborhood's population was then racially mixed, during Reconstruction Jackson Ward served as the center of Richmond's black community. By the end of World War I, Jackson Ward was predominantly black, and has remained so ever since.[84]

Although Jackson Ward makes up roughly one-quarter of the central core of Richmond, after 1920 both city officials and private investors began to ignore the neighborhood, which then entered a sharp and prolonged decline. For the past fifty years Jackson Ward has been one of Richmond's poorest neighborhoods. In 1975 its unemployment rate was double the city's, and the median income for Jackson Ward families was $4,948, compared to $8,673 citywide. Of all households in Jackson Ward, 23 percent received welfare in 1975, and 35.5 percent had female heads. In 1974, Jackson Ward had the highest crime rate in Richmond. Moreover, Jackson Ward has always suffered from problems stemming from its proximity to Richmond's central business district. A great deal of traffic in and out of the city is routed through Jackson Ward.

Jackson Ward's housing stock, most of which was built between 1860 and 1910, can be divided into two categories. The residential buildings in Old Jackson Ward, the original freedmen's area, are mostly small wooden cottages. In the area incorporating Broad and Leigh streets the homes are generally large brick structures of Federal, Greek revival, or Italianate style. Many of these homes have distinctive cast-iron porches. In recent decades the vast majority of Jackson Ward's homes have fallen into extreme disrepair. In 1975 more than 90 percent of the homes in the area needed at least minor repairs, and 9.8 percent of Jackson Ward's residential structures lacked indoor plumbing.

In 1979 Richmond city officials and the news media began to notice that a number of middle-income households were buying homes in Jackson Ward. While Jackson Ward's convenient location and its spacious, historic homes may have helped lure these inmovers, undoubtedly their primary motivation was economic. From 1970 to 1976 the median sales price for a home in Jackson Ward hovered between $5,000 and $10,000. Many resources were (and still are) available to aid middle-income households interested in buying homes in Jackson Ward. Both city and federal governments have low-interest mortgage plans for historic conservation areas such as parts of Jackson Ward. There is also a special state mortgage program for families with incomes of between $22,000 and $28,000.[85] Historic Richmond, an organization devoted to preserving parts of Richmond's architec-

89

tural heritage, has acquired, restored, and renovated a number of homes in Jackson Ward.[86]

The 1980 census confirms the increase in Jackson Ward's white population, although the neighborhood's population is still overwhelmingly black. Racial figures, however, are not necessarily good indicators of revitalization in Jackson Ward, since many of the neighborhood's middle-income inmovers are black. These homebuyers include some blacks moving into Richmond from out of town, as well as consortiums of doctors who have attracted a great deal of attention from the local news media.[87]

Far better indicators of the extent of revitalization in the neighborhood can be found in the Polk figures on our study area, the historic conservation area in Jackson Ward's southern half (see table 16). According to Polk data, between 1973-1974 and 1979-1980 the percentage of households with three or more children decreased from 34.7 to 19.3, while the percentage of one-person households increased from 33.0 to 55.0. The percentage of units with professional or managerial heads went from 12.9 in 1973-1974 to 24.8 in 1979-1980, another sign of revitalization. Two other indicators, the percentage of female-headed households with children and the percentage of retired heads of households, did not change in the direction one would expect in a revitalizing neighborhood. The reason for this is not immediately apparent.

The figures on housing sales in the study area also indicate a trend toward revitalization during the late seventies (see table 17). Between 1970 and 1979 the number of home sales nearly tripled and the median sales price nearly doubled. During the first eight months of 1980, the median sales price in Jackson Ward was $20,000. Local observers predict that the neighborhood's revitalization will continue, although it may not accelerate greatly. According to Jean Boyea, head of the city's community development department, two main factors prevent more rapid revitalization. First, the overall state of the economy has brought about a lull in revitalization activity throughout Richmond. Second, the neighborhood's negative image as the city's worst crime area scares away some prospective inmovers and investors.[88]

Local black officials and community leaders have expressed some concern over displacement in Jackson Ward.[89] Many local observers, however, feel that because of the slow pace of revitalization the problem is not significant. In any case, neighborhood groups have not yet made a concerted effort either to study or to combat displacement in Jackson Ward.

Table 16 CHARACTERISTICS OF JACKSON WARD HOUSEHOLDS

	ALL H/HOLDS	OUT-MOVERS	IN-MOVERS	ALL OCC. H/HOLDS
1973–1974				
Percentage of owner-occupied units	25.9	16.7	6.6	29.1
Percentage of female-headed households with children	7.2	10.4	11.5	7.5
Percentage of households with 3 or more children	34.8	36.4	27.9	34.7
Percentage of single-person households	31.6	27.3	49.2	33.0
Percentage of units with professional or managerial head of households	12.5	18.5	27.3	12.9
(sample size)	(263)	(27)	(11)	(217)
Percentage of retired head of households	20.5	9.1	11.5	22.2
Sample size	643	77	61	464
1976–1977				
Percentage of owner-occupied units	15.7	10.5	4.5	17.7
Percentage of female-headed households with children	7.8	12.6	3.0	5.8
Percentage of households with 3 or more children	21.2	23.2	13.4	21.3
Percentage of single-person households	51.7	47.4	76.1	51.7
Percentage of units with professional or managerial head of households	20.9	11.5	21.1	23.3
(sample size)	(211)	(26)	(19)	(176)
Percentage of retired head of households	32.8	28.4	17.9	34.1
Sample size	725	127	67	464
1979–1980				
Percentage of owner-occupied units	16.9	3.0	5.5	22.3
Percentage of female-headed households with children	7.3	6.6	4.4	8.6
Percentage of households with 3 or more children	17.5	12.1	7.7	19.3
Percentage of single-person households	51.3	47.5	58.2	55.0

Table 16 cont'd

Percentage of units with professional or managerial head of households (sample size)ᵃ	22.1 (131)	7.7 (13)	33.3 (9)	24.8 (109)
Percentage of retired head of households	29.5	15.2	9.9	35.7
Sample size	644	136	91	373

Source: Computed from canvass files by R. L. Polk & Company.
a. Sample sizes for occupation indicator are smaller than for other indicators.

Table 17 HOUSE SALES IN JACKSON WARD

YEAR	NUMBER OF SALES	MEDIAN SALES PRICE	MEDIAN SALES PRICE IN 1967 DOLLARS
1970	11	$9,475	$8,009
1973	33	6,900	5,200
1976	20	10,050	5,968
1979	30	18,000	8,068

Source: Richmond City Assessor's Office.

Oregon Hill. Oregon Hill is a small, relatively low-density neighborhood located on a plateau immediately west of downtown Richmond. The neighborhood's borders—the James River on the south, a cemetery on the west, a highway on the east, and an expressway on the north—isolate it physically from the rest of the city.[90]

Most of Oregon Hill's housing stock was constructed between 1840 and 1890 for single-family use, with infill housing constructed between 1890 and 1915. Virtually all the neighborhood's structures were built before 1950. In recent years some of the buildings have been demolished, but those that remain are in fairly good condition.

Historically, Oregon Hill's population has been primarily lower-income white families. In 1970, 81.5 percent of the employed persons in Oregon Hill were blue-collar workers, and 91.5 percent of the neighborhood's residents were white. The median family income in Oregon Hill that year was $5,962, while the citywide figure was $8,673. Approximately 28 percent of the households in Oregon Hill were owner-occupied, with the remainder rented out at a median contract rent of $64 a month as opposed to a $78 median citywide. While the neighborhood has generally been on the low end of the socioeconomic scale—in 1970, 23.2 percent of its families were below the poverty level compared with 17.5 percent citywide—Oregon Hill is by no means a deteriorating community. With an average crime rate less than one-fifth that of Jackson Ward, crime has not been a significant problem in the neighborhood.

Recently, there has been some evidence of revitalization in Oregon Hill. The adjacent Fan District has undergone extensive revitalization and the prices of homes are escalating rapidly. While Oregon Hill's homes are not nearly as attractive or substantial as the three-story brick and masonry single-family homes in the Fan District, they are affordable for the many prospective homeowners priced out of the Fan, and local real estate firms have begun to advertise Oregon Hill as the "South Fan." Oregon Hill also borders on Virginia Commonwealth University, and in the past few years university students have begun to rent apartments in the area. Recent small-scale public improvement projects in Oregon Hill may further attract higher-income inmovers. As yet, however, neither public nor private sources have made significant investments in the neighborhood.[91]

Overall, Polk data on Oregon Hill do not indicate that the neighborhood underwent dramatic change between 1973–1974 and 1970–1980 (see table 18). While the proportion of female-headed households with children decreased slightly during this period, the percentage of one-person households and retired heads of households remained relatively constant. Units with professional or managerial heads did increase from 15.2 percent of all households in 1973–1974 to 20.0 percent in 1980.

Housing sales data indicate that the Oregon Hill housing market is experiencing a mild upsurge (see table 19). Both median sales price and numbers of sales spurted in 1972, and again after 1977. The large increase in number of sales between 1976 and 1979 is at least partly attributable to the sale of groups of buildings as parcels to investors.[92] It remains to be seen whether market pressures will increase and raise housing prices higher in Oregon Hill or whether demand will slacken.

Oregon Hill residents are worried that Virginia Commonwealth University may expand and displace neighborhood residents. A few years ago the university bought several parcels of land covering almost two blocks in order to build a student athletic complex. The move met with strong community opposition, which included picketing and the posting of signs in front of homes indicating that they were not for sale.[93]

93

Table 18 CHARACTERISTICS OF OREGON HILL HOUSEHOLDS

	ALL H/HOLDS	OUT-MOVERS	IN-MOVERS	ALL OCC. H/HOLDS
1973–1974				
Percentage of owner-occupied units	19.6	11.3	5.9	21.3
Percentage of female-headed households with children	7.0	9.7	2.9	7.4
Percentage of households with 3 or more children	21.7	27.0	5.9	22.5
Percentage of single-person households	46.0	45.3	79.4	45.5
Percentage of units with professional or managerial head of households	21.2	21.7	0.0	15.2
(sample size)[a]	(156)	(23)	(10)	(178)
Percentage of retired head of households	31.5	26.4	23.5	33.0
Sample size	497	62	34	367
1976–1977				
Percentage of owner-occupied units	24.5	9.2	3.3	28.9
Percentage of female-headed households with children	5.8	9.5	4.4	5.7
Percentage of households with 3 or more children	28.0	38.5	18.7	26.1
Percentage of single-person households	44.2	40.4	63.7	44.8
Percentage of units with professional or managerial head of households	17.6	34.3	20.0	19.7
(sample size)[a]	(256)	(35)	(20)	(213)
Percentage of retired head of households	27.7	21.1	4.4	30.3
Sample size	765	137	91	505
1979–1980				
Percentage of owner-occupied units	23.7	13.7	11.9	26.5
Percentage of female-headed households with children	5.4	4.8	3.7	5.7
Percentage of households with 3 or more children	14.3	29.4	20.9	24.3

Table 18 cont'd

Percentage of single- person households	47.8	54.9	58.2	45.7
Percentage of units with professional or managerial head of households	20.5	24.5	21.3	20.0
(sample size)ª	(263)	(49)	(47)	(205)
Percentage of retired head of households	29.2	14.7	9.7	32.4
Sample size	791	124	134	784

Source: Computed from canvass files by R. L. Polk & Company.
a. Sample sizes for occupation indicator are smaller than for other indicators.

Table 19 HOUSE SALES IN OREGON HILL

YEAR	NUMBER OF SALES	MEDIAN SALES PRICE	MEDIAN SALES PRICE IN 1967 DOLLARS
1970	17	$ 2,500	$2,113
1973	36	5,250	3,956
1976	18	6,500	3,860
1979	40	11,000	4,931

Source: Richmond City Assessor's Office.

Seattle

Since 1960, Seattle's population has been in a state of flux. Between 1960 and 1977, the population of the Seattle-Everett SMSA increased by a third, from 1,103,000 to 1,427,000. The population of the city itself, however, decreased by 11.4 percent from 1960 to 1980, dropping from 557,087 to 493,846.[94] During this same period the city's minority population increased sharply. Between 1970 and 1980 the number of blacks in Seattle increased by one-quarter and the number of Asians and Pacific Islanders jumped by over 60 percent. In addition, Seattle recently absorbed a major influx of Asian boat people.[95]

Seattle's economy is linked to the airplane industry and, more specifically, to the Boeing Company. Boeing laid off more than 60 percent of its workers during 1969–1970.[96] This left the entire Seattle area in a depression that, among other things, stimulated a net outflow of population and depressed residential values and real estate activity. During the second half of the seventies, the firm steadily rebuilt its business and has until recently been thriving. The Boeing resurgence, combined with the success of many businesses established during the firm's earlier decline, have made Seattle's economy one of the most active of American cities.[97] After completion of data

95

collection for this study, the economy of Seattle appeared to decline again due to the effect of the recession on Boeing and the Washington lumber industry.

Seattle's economic renaissance attracted many newcomers. Between 1974 and 1979, 30,000 households—15 percent of all households currently residing in Seattle—moved into the city from outside the SMSA.[98] This major influx of population combined with a sharp decline in average household size—one-third of the city's households are single-person ones[99]—places extraordinary pressure on the city's housing market. These pressures are felt all the more acutely because of the housing depression of the early 1970s. The vacancy rate for single-family homes, the predominant form of housing in the city, stood at 1.8 percent in 1980. (It has not been above 2 percent since April 1975.)[100] The rate for multifamily dwellings was 2.11 percent.[101] Seattle has recently experienced great inflation of housing prices. Between 1976 and 1981, the average sales price for a home in Seattle increased more than 29 percent per year.[102]

Much of the housing demand is focused on the city's downtown neighborhoods, half of which have been rebuilt since 1970.[103] Residential reinvestment is widespread in downtown neighborhoods, even those that are not particularly distinctive or attractive.

Mann-Minor. The Mann-Minor neighborhood, located immediately to the east of Seattle's central business district, is part of the city's larger Central Area neighborhood, synonymous with the black community in Seattle.[104] Ever since Mann-Minor's undistinctive, medium-sized one- and two-family homes were built in the 1930s and 1940s, they have been inhabited by working-class families. Since 1945, the neighborhood has been predominantly black.

Throughout the sixties and the seventies, Mann-Minor was one of Seattle's most blighted neighborhoods. A 1974 citywide study classified it as having the worst housing conditions in Seattle.[105] Over the years Mann-Minor received large amounts of government funds earmarked for revitalization. Part of the neighborhood was designated an urban renewal area in the 1960s.[106]

Toward the end of the 1970s, local observers began to realize that, for all its problems, Mann-Minor was on the verge of becoming the site of significant revitalization, primarily by individual middle- and upper-class inmovers. The neighborhood's convenient central-city location was no doubt a major contributor to Mann-Minor's sudden desirability, but other newer features were also responsible for its resurgence. Mann-Minor had a significantly higher vacancy rate than most of Seattle's older neighborhoods, so it could more readily accommodate inmovers suffering from the city's otherwise severe housing crunch.[107] Also, Mann-Minor's eastern neighbor, Capitol Hill, had been one of the first neighborhoods in the city to undergo revitalization. By the middle of the last decade, Capitol Hill was almost fully revitalized and its homes were quite expensive, leading some households to search in Mann-Minor for homes.[108]

A local community development organization, the Madison-Jackson Economic Development Council (MAD-JAC), has been relatively successful in attracting outside, private investment to the neighborhood. MAD-JAC also sponsored a home improvement contest in the neighborhood, which led to the rehabilitation of more than eighty homes. Other residential rehabilitation has also been actively undertaken by both owner-occupants and investors in recent years. A 1978 citywide housing study noted that, while Mann-Minor's housing conditions were still among the worst in the city, the rate of improvement was among the highest.[109] At the same time, as table 20 indicates, both the demand for Mann-Minor homes and median sales prices have risen dramatically.

Census figures serve as an even more dramatic signal that Mann-Minor underwent revitalization during the 1970s. In 1970 the study area was 50 percent black, but by 1980 it was only 39 percent black.[110] According to a neighborhood planning official, the 1980 figure reflects a decline that began only in the past few years, and indicates the beginning of an accelerating trend.[111] Polk data indicate that Mann-Minor's household composition is also undergoing significant change (see table 21). In 1973–1974, 26.1 percent of the neighborhood's households identified themselves as having professional or managerial heads. By 1979–1980, this percentage had increased to 38.5. Other Polk indicators show a similar pattern.

Table 20 HOUSE SALES IN MANN-MINOR

YEAR	NUMBER OF SALES	MEDIAN SALES PRICE	MEDIAN SALES PRICE IN 1967 DOLLARS
1970	4	$13,750	$11,623
1973	6	21,050	14,398
1976	14	18,425	10,607
1979	31	45,000	19,430

Source: King County Assessor's Office.

97

Table 21 CHARACTERISTICS OF MANN-MINOR HOUSEHOLDS

	ALL H/HOLDS	OUT-MOVERS	IN-MOVERS	ALL OCC. H/HOLDS
1973–1974				
Percentage of owner-occupied units	21.2	7.5	2.8	25.9
Percentage of female-headed households with children	4.6	3.5	1.7	5.8
Percentage of households with 3 or more children	14.4	7.8	2.8	16.6
Percentage of single-person households	67.6	79.6	89.4	63.7
Percentage of units with professional or managerial head of households	29.5	45.3	55.1	26.1
(sample size)	(810)	(95)	(49)	(690)
Percentage of retired head of households	14.6	11.5	5.3	15.4
Sample size	3,762	937	530	2,243
1976–1977				
Percentage of owner-occupied units	21.8	8.5	4.2	24.1
Percentage of female-headed households with children	3.7	1.6	0.7	4.7
Percentage of households with 3 or more children	13.3	4.9	2.1	14.6
Percentage of single-person households	68.5	80.5	87.4	66.5
Percentage of units with professional or managerial head of households	29.3	36.8	58.3	28.0
(sample size)	(740)	(57)	(36)	(671)
Percentage of retired head of households	11.8	7.9	1.6	12.4
Sample size	3,773	512	430	2,724
1979–1980				
Percentage of owner-occupied units	13.1	6.9	6.0	16.7
Percentage of female-headed households with children	3.9	2.0	2.7	5.2
Percentage of households with 3 or more children	10.6	8.8	8.8	11.8
Percentage of single-person households	70.4	73.4	73.9	68.1

Table 21 cont'd

Percentage of units with professional or managerial head of households (sample size)[a]	40.3 (226)	42.6 (61)	44.1 (59)	38.5 (153)
Percentage of retired head of households	7.8	3.0	3.8	10.8
Sample size	1,410	503	402	762

Source: Computed from canvass files by R. L. Polk & Company.
a. Sample sizes for occupation indicator are smaller than for other indicators.

The direction Mann-Minor's future should take has stirred up some controversy. The neighborhood still has large tracts of vacant land. Some neighborhood leaders would like to see lower-income housing on this land, while private developers are eager to use it for market-rate housing.[112]

Some concern about displacement in Mann-Minor has been expressed. In an interview with the *Seattle Times* in 1978, Jerome Page, then executive director of the Seattle Urban League, said that displacement of blacks from the Central Area was taking place at an appalling rate.[113] The Central Area Citizens Housing Committee has drawn up proposals to assist low- and moderate-income homeowners in the area.[114]

North Beacon Hill. Until the 1940s, the North Beacon Hill neighborhood, a short distance from Seattle's central business district, consisted of scattered truck farms. During the 1940s, small, low-cost one- and two-story frame houses were built there, and today 88 percent of the structures in the study area are single-family detached homes.[115] The neighborhood enjoys a view and is only minutes from downtown by car or public transportation.[116]

North Beacon Hill has generally been a lower-middle-income area. The neighborhood's racial and ethnic makeup has changed considerably during the past fifteen years. According to a 1977 Community Development Planning Report on North Beacon Hill, "Although there has been a large exodus of white families from the neighborhood over the last 10–15 years, there has been a yet larger inmigration of other ethnic groups."[117] This same report estimated that North Beacon Hill's racial or ethnic composition in 1977 was 47 percent white, 15 percent Chinese, 15 percent Japanese, 14 percent black, and 9 percent other nonwhite. More recently, the neighborhood has become home to a large group of Indochinese refugees.

99

Major public and private sources of funds have so far bypassed North Beacon Hill. The neighborhood was not an urban renewal area, although in the late 1970s it did receive some city funds for street improvements. Some local observers have noted individual middle- and upper-income inmovers entering North Beacon Hill. Certain evidence indicates that the neighborhood's socioeconomic composition may indeed be changing. According to the Polk data for the study area, which consists of the northern tip of the neighborhood, in 1976–1977, 60.0 percent of all inmoving households had professional or managerial heads, while only 40.3 percent of all outmoving households were employed in these high-income positions (see table 22). But most of Polk's indexes of household composition do not indicate a major change in North Beacon Hill's socioeconomic makeup. This may be because residential revitalization in the neighborhood is sporadic, taking place house by house rather than block by block.

Housing sales data for the study area indicate that during the second half of the 1970s, the demand for housing in the neighborhood increased (see table 23).

Recent developments may determine the future of North Beacon Hill. A group of private developers has proposed building a seventy-unit condominium on vacant land in the neighborhood.[118] Should the plans go through, a sizable number of middle- and upper-income households presumably will move into the area. On the other hand, the neighborhood has been involved in zoning fights in recent years, and many of the high-rise zones have been abolished.[119] Perhaps the most crucial decision affecting the future of North Beacon Hill is the Reagan administration's proposed closing of the Public Health Service hospital on the neighborhood's northern tip. The hospital closing could slow neighborhood development and cost the area many jobs.[120]

Conclusion

Despite their diverse housing stocks, the variations in their ethnic, racial, and economic makeup, and the different forces that sparked the inmigration of higher-income households, the neighborhoods examined in this study share several characteristics. Each has experienced an increase in the numbers of newcomer households purchasing and renovating homes in recent years. This population change is frequently, although not always, observable by analyzing census

Methodology and Description of Study Areas

Table 22 CHARACTERISTICS OF NORTH BEACON HILL HOUSEHOLDS

	ALL H/HOLDS	OUT-MOVERS	IN-MOVERS	ALL OCC. H/HOLDS
1973–1974				
Percentage of owner-occupied units	18.9	5.1	3.4	22.9
Percentage of female-headed households with children	4.5	3.9	4.8	4.8
Percentage of households with 3 or more children	18.6	16.7	6.2	18.5
Percentage of single-person households	61.2	67.1	74.5	60.2
Percentage of units with professional or managerial head of households	36.8	37.7	39.3	36.1
(sample size)[a]	(307)	(53)	(28)	(247)
Percentage of retired head of households	9.6	1.4	1.9	11.7
Sample size	1,227	282	208	821
1976–1977				
Percentage of owner-occupied units	7.5	2.5	0.6	8.7
Percentage of female-headed households with children	2.9	3.3	0.9	2.8
Percentage of households with 3 or more children	8.2	4.6	1.8	9.0
Percentage of single-person households	75.7	78.5	91.2	75.2
Percentage of units with professional or managerial head of households	43.5	40.3	60.0	49.0
(sample size)[a]	(324)	(72)	(25)	(248)
Percentage of retired head of households	9.0	6.1	1.5	9.7
Sample size	1,748	366	341	1,265
1979–1980				
Percentage of owner-occupied units	15.2	7.2	5.4	17.9
Percentage of female-headed households with children	3.1	2.2	3.2	3.5
Percentage of households with 3 or more children	12.2	8.4	8.5	13.5
Percentage of single-person households	70.3	75.7	77.6	68.2

Table 22 cont'd

Percentage of units with professional or managerial head of households	32.9	30.3	19.5	34.1
(sample size)[a]	(273)	(66)	(41)	(205)
Percentage of retired head of households	16.0	11.5	2.8	17.8
Sample size	1,438	363	317	978

Source: Computed from canvass files by R. L. Polk & Company.
a. Sample sizes for occupation indicator are smaller than for other indicators.

Table 23 HOUSE SALES IN NORTH BEACON HILL

YEAR	NUMBER OF SALES	MEDIAN SALES PRICE	MEDIAN SALES PRICE IN 1967 DOLLARS
1970	4	$12,625	$10,672
1973	10	16,500	11,286
1976	11	13,250	7,628
1979	16	39,500	17,055

Source: King County Assessor's Office.

or Polk indicators on neighborhood change. The two indicators that consistently document the renewed interest in the housing stock of these neighborhoods are the rise in the number of house sales and the rise in the median sales prices that have occurred over the past decade.

Each of these neighborhoods is primarily made up of rental units, although the shape, size, and architectural styles differ from city to city and indeed from neighborhood to neighborhood. Each of the study areas chosen is relatively close to the central business district of its city. In addition, each of these areas still contained a significant proportion of lower-income households in 1979—households that could be subject to displacement as the neighborhood proceeds to revitalize. As we have already mentioned, we have avoided choosing neighborhoods in which reinvestment would be most obvious or easily documented, since the low-income population in those neighborhoods would already have been significantly reduced. These neighborhoods are not Society Hills; in fact, many would still be characterized by city residents as deteriorated. They are, however, areas in which reinvestment activity has begun and may well continue.

CHAPTER 5

Results of the Displacement Study

In order for policymakers to develop a rational public response to the problem of displacement, they must first know certain basic facts about the process and its effects on those involved. What is the magnitude of displacement in revitalizing neighborhoods? Are any particular socioeconomic or racial groups more susceptible to being displaced than others? Do displaced households encounter significant hardships attributable to displacement? Finally, are any identifiable subgroups of the displaced population in need of special help due to especially severe hardships?

To learn the answers to these and other questions, we conducted the survey of renters who moved out of nine neighborhoods described in chapter 4. For the most part, the results for the sample of displaced households are compared with the responses of nondisplaced (voluntary) movers. Occasionally, when it is useful to disaggregate the responses of the voluntary movers, we will examine those who moved for an employment-related reason, for a better house or neighborhood, and for reasons relating to a change in housing needs. Disaggregated data for these categories of voluntary movers appear in appendix D.

Several indices of socioeconomic and racial status were examined to learn whether particular population groups were negatively affected by displacement. We expected that certain segments of the population would be more likely to be displaced than others. Since displacement frequently occurs under conditions where housing costs rise more rapidly than income, low-income households were expected to constitute a large proportion of the displaced households. We also expected that particular populations whose members earned low incomes would therefore be more likely to be displaced—the elderly, racial minorities, the unemployed, and households composed of persons with limited educational backgrounds and employment experience.

103

By means of the study, we sought to determine whether displaced households became worse off as a result of being displaced. Despite some empirical evidence to the contrary,[1] we expected that displaced households would, as a group, encounter difficulties. The sudden and forced nature of their move, the limited resources upon which they could draw, and in some cases the tight housing markets in which they were forced to search for new housing might well cause hardship. As discussed in the previous chapter, hardship was rated by both objective measures (e.g., increased rent, crowding, commuting times) and subjective indicators (such as the outmover's evaluation of the new home and neighborhood compared with the old ones).

Moreover, it was expected that displaced households would, on the average, react more negatively to their move than households that moved voluntarily. The latter would presumably be moving to new and better homes, whereas displaced households might be forced to take whatever accommodations they could find. As the most vulnerable members of the community, displaced households might find their choices more limited than those who moved voluntarily.

Finally, within the displaced population we expected certain groups would encounter greater hardships than others. Those households with the least financial resources and fewest capabilities needed to cope with a sudden and forced change in life-style would be likely to encounter the greatest difficulty in finding new homes that they would be satisfied with. Among those groups we suspected would be most vulnerable are those who earn the lowest income, the elderly, and those who had the least education. In addition we expected that the choices of racial minorities would be narrowed due to discrimination within the housing market.

Why Do Households Move?

Of the reasons for moving specified on the questionnaire, the one most frequently chosen by respondents as their major reason for moving was a desire for a better house (see table 24). This reason was chosen by sixty households or 12 percent of the entire sample of 507 outmovers. The second most popular reason for moving was a rise in rents, which was given by fifty-seven households or 11 percent of the sample. Other frequently selected reasons for moving were the need for a larger home and the desire to own one's own home, each cited by fifty-six households. We grouped the eighteen responses on the questionnaire into six summary categories:

104

Table 24 REASONS FOR MOVING

REASON	PERCENTAGE OF HOUSEHOLDS
Desired better house	11.8
Rent increase	11.2
Needed larger house	11.0
Wanted to own home	11.0
Desired better neighborhood	9.9
Evicted because of renovation or conversion	6.3
Home sold by landlord	5.3
Change in marital status	4.1
Job transfer	3.2
Wanted to live closer to job	3.0
Wanted to live closer to relatives	2.0
To begin own household	1.8
Needed smaller home	1.4
Retired	0.8
To attend school	0.8
Want to rent home	0.8
Natural disaster	0.8
Want to live closer to better school	0.4
Miscellaneous	14.4

a. Uncodable reasons for moving (N = 73) not included.

- Displacement, as defined in chapter 4
- Job-related
- Change in housing needs
- Wanted better house
- Wanted better neighborhood
- Other reasons for moving

The largest number of outmovers, as grouped in these summary categories, moved because of a change in housing needs, induced by a change in household size or composition, the desire to own or rent a house, or the desire to begin their own households. Thirty percent of the sample chose this reason for moving. The second most frequently chosen explanation for moving, given by 23 percent of the respondents, was displacement resulting from increased rents and from eviction due to conversion, house sale, or renovation. Other categories contained much smaller portions of the sample.

Displacement Rates for Individual Neighborhoods

Except for the two neighborhoods at the high and low extremes, most of the neighborhoods studied had similar rates of displacement, ranging from 17 to 22 percent of all households moving from rented accommodations. Of the nine neighborhoods examined, Denver's Baker had the highest rate—almost 40 percent (see table 25). The lowest rate, 8 percent, was found in Richmond's Jackson Ward.

What Characteristics Do Displaced and Voluntary Movers Share?

In table 26 a summary of some socioeconomic and racial characteristics frequently used when comparing displaced and nondisplaced movers are presented. In some cases the proportions are compatible with popular conceptions of displaced households, while in others the findings are surprising.

Size of Household and Marital Status

Displaced households tended to be smaller than those that moved for other reasons. When voluntary movers were considered as a group, the proportion of single-person households in that group was not statistically different from the proportion of single-person households in the displaced group. Despite this fact, when the voluntary movers were disaggregated by reason for moving (see appendix D), single-person households were more prominently represented in the displaced group than they were in all other categories of movers, except those who moved for an employment-related reason. This was probably due to the number of college students who were included in this category of movers.

Table 25 NEIGHBORHOOD DISPLACEMENT RATES

NEIGHBORHOOD	DISPLACEMENT RATE	SAMPLE SIZE
North End (Boston)	21	67
South End (Boston)	21	62
Corryville (Cincinnati)	22	74
Mulberry (Cincinnati)	17	23
Baker (Denver)	39	82
Oregon Hill (Richmond)	21	34
Jackson Ward (Richmond)	8	25
Mann-Minor (Seattle)	19	64
North Beacon Hill (Seattle)	21	76

Table 26 SOCIOECONOMIC CHARACTERISTICS OF MOVERS

CHARACTERISTIC	NONDISPLACED MOVERS (PERCENTAGE)	DISPLACED (PERCENTAGE)	T-RATIO
Over sixty-five years of age	11	14	0.84
Female-headed	33	33	0.00
Married	48	36	2.34
Nonwhite	43	46	0.57
Black	20	22	0.46
Hispanic	5	14	2.64
Asian	17	8	2.85
Unemployed	4	18	3.78
Completed 12th grade	75	63	2.40
Income under $10,000	29	50	4.06
Income over $25,000	18	6	4.08
Single-person households	25	34	1.83
Had lived in neighborhood more than 5 years	35	36	0.20
Sample size	391	116	

Note: The t-ratio is a statistic used to test the null hypothesis that there is no difference between the two percentages with which it is associated. A t-ratio of greater than 1.96 leads us to reject the null hypothesis and to conclude that there is a statistical difference between the two proportions.

Just over one-third of the displaced households were married, compared with almost half of the voluntary movers. The displaced had a smaller proportion of married couples than any category of the voluntary movers. This may provide a partial explanation for why the displaced households' size was smaller than that of voluntary movers.

Sex, Age, and Race

Although the proportion of households with a head of household aged sixty-five years or older was greater for the displaced group (14 percent) than it was for the nondisplaced group (11 percent), these differences were not statistically significant. Also the proportion of households that had lived in the study neighborhoods for more than five years was not significantly different in either sample—just over one-third in each group. These findings are surprising in the light of popular claims that displacement uproots long-term residents and places a great burden on the aged.

A third of all households were headed by females in both the displaced and the nondisplaced samples. This is somewhat surprising. One would expect displaced households to have lower incomes, and female-headed households—especially those with dependent children—are frequently found at the lower-income levels. As a result, one would expect them to be disproportionately represented in the displaced group. One explanation for the statistical similarity between the two groups might be that this category also includes households with no children.

When all nonwhites were grouped together, it was found that they were similarly represented in each group. Forty-three percent of the voluntary movers were nonwhite compared to 46 percent of the displaced. However, when this group was disaggregated further, one finds that the racial composition of the two groups is quite different. Fourteen percent of the displaced had Hispanic heads of household compared with only 5 percent of the voluntary movers.[2] On the other hand, although only 8 percent of the displaced sample were Asians, 17 percent of the nondisplaced households had an Asian head. The proportion of blacks in each group was not statistically different— 22 percent for the displaced and 20 percent for the nondisplaced.

Income and Education

As expected, displaced households had lower incomes than did households that moved for other reasons. Overall, half the displaced households had incomes of less than $10,000 per year. Among non-displaced households, only 29 percent had such low incomes. Similarly, only 6 percent of displaced households earned incomes of $25,000 or more per year, but among nondisplaced households triple that rate earned that much or more. Within the nondisplaced sample, those who moved in order to obtain better housing had the lowest incomes, while those who moved for reasons of employment had the highest. In order to control for household size, we computed the proportion of households whose incomes were under the poverty level for the displaced and nondisplaced samples.[3] The percentage was 31 percent for displaced households, and only 13 percent for the nondisplaced outmovers.

Members of displaced households were less likely than nondisplaced outmovers to have completed high school. Sixty-three percent of displaced heads of households had completed high school (twelfth grade) compared with three-quarters of the voluntary outmovers. In the nondisplaced sample, those who moved because of a change in employment status had the highest levels of education, while those who moved to acquire a better house or neighborhood had the lowest.

108

Displacement Rates among Different Population Groups

Another way to examine the characteristics of displaced households is to compare displacement rates for various populations (see table 27). Overall the displacement rate for the entire population of out-movers from the nine neighborhoods was 23 percent. Among non-whites generally, the displacement rate was 25 percent, which is not statistically different from the overall rate. However, for both Hispanics and Asians, the displacement rates were statistically different from the overall average. Hispanics had a higher displacement rate, and the rate for Asians was lower than the average.

Displacement rates increased rapidly as income declined. For all households earning over $25,000 per year, the percentage displaced was only 9, but it rose to 45 percent for those with incomes below $5,000. At the two ends of the income spectrum, the displacement rate was statistically different from the average. At the upper end the rate was lower, while at the bottom end the rate was significantly

Table 27 DISPLACEMENT RATES FOR VARIOUS POPULATIONS

CATEGORY	PERCENTAGE DISPLACED	SAMPLE SIZE	T-RATIO
Overall	23	507	
Whites	22	282	0.32
Nonwhites	25	216	0.57
Blacks	25	100	0.42
Hispanics	47	34	2.74
Asians	12	75	2.62
Over sixty-five years of age	27	60	0.66
Income: 0–$4,999	45	60	3.29
$5,000–$9,999	29	84	1.13
$10,000–$14,999	27	94	0.81
$15,000–$19,999	18	61	0.95
$20,000–$24,999	15	60	1.61
$25,000 and above	9	65	3.49
Did not complete high school education	31	134	1.81
Married	18	226	1.58
One-person household	28	137	1.17
Moved more than 4 times in last ten years	26	149	0.74
Households with more than 4 persons	27	66	0.69

Note: The t-ratio is used to test the null hypothesis that there is no difference between the proportion displaced in the entire sample and the proportion for each subgroup presented. A t-ratio greater than 1.96 is enough to reject the null hypothesis.

higher. Although 31 percent of the households with a head who had not completed high school were displaced, this proportion was not significantly different from the overall average.

The displacement rate for all other population groups investigated was not statistically different from the average. Surprisingly, households headed by elderly individuals, transient households, and relatively large households were not particularly likely to be displaced.

Do Any Characteristics Predict Displacement?

The statistical analysis presented in the previous two sections is descriptive: It describes the characteristics of displaced households relative to voluntary movers. In order to learn which characteristics are causally related to the likelihood that a given household will be displaced, we conducted a probit analysis in which the dependent variable represented whether or not the household was displaced. (For a detailed description of the development of the model, see the appendix to this chapter.) Among the independent or explanatory variables that we examined were the race and sex of the household head, the age of the household head, the size of the household, the household head's marital status, the frequency with which the household had moved in the previous ten years, the monthly rent in the housing unit from which the household moved, the employment status of the household head, whether the household lived in a large apartment building, and the income and education levels of the household head. The equation that shows the final product of the probit analysis is presented in table 28.

Only those variables that displayed a significant power in explaining displacement are included in the model presented here. This equation

Table 28 DISPLACEMENT MODEL FOR ALL HOUSEHOLDS

INDEPENDENT VARIABLES	CONSTANT	FEMHD3	UNEMP	HISPAN	INCOME	SINGLE
Coefficient estimate	−0.99	0.40	0.35	0.66	−0.03[a]	0.48
T-ratio	(4.71)	(2.33)	(2.36)	(2.83)	(3.48)	(3.25)

Note: See the appendix to this chapter for specific codes for variables used in these tables.
a. This coefficient represents the effect of a change of $1,000 in the household's income.

best summarizes the information available from the data. The model shows that Hispanic-headed households are most likely to be displaced.[4] As previously noted, a large proportion of the Hispanics included in the study were found in the sample from the Baker neighborhood in Denver, where a disproportionate amount of displacement relative to the other neighborhoods occurred. The correlation between these two observations may be responsible for this result.

The population groups next most likely to be displaced were single-person households, female-headed households, and those with an unemployed member. The final explanatory variable was the household's income. The negative sign on the income variable indicates that the propensity of a household to be displaced falls as income increases. This is reasonable, since one would expect households to be more able to afford increases in their rent as their incomes increase.

Contrary to our expectations, we found no significant correlation between the fact that a household was headed by an elderly or black person and the likelihood that the household would be displaced.

Where Do Displaced Households Relocate?

Changes in zip codes were used as a rough index of how far households moved from their previous home. As table 29 shows, for the most part displaced households do not move so far from their previous homes as do voluntary movers.[5] Over 70 percent of the displaced households, and 60 percent of the voluntary movers, moved to homes with the same zip code or into an adjacent postal zone. Only 8 percent of the displaced, but 17 percent of the voluntary movers moved to homes in the city's suburbs or out of the metropolitan area.

For our sample in general, displaced households were more likely to move to a neighborhood close to their original neighborhoods than were nondisplaced movers. The only exception to this generalization was in Boston, where, although a majority (53 percent) of displaced households remained in the same or adjacent postal zones, a slightly larger portion (54 percent) of voluntary movers also located nearby. Even so, a larger proportion of voluntary than displaced movers left Boston.

Table 29 DISTANCE MOVED

CITY	MOVED WITHIN POSTAL ZONE	MOVED TO ADJACENT POSTAL ZONE	MOVED TO SOME OTHER LOCATION IN CITY	MOVED OUT OF CITY
Boston				
Displaced	47.1	5.9	23.5	23.5
Nondisplaced	40.8	13.2	15.8	30.3
Cincinnati				
Displaced	45.5	27.3	27.3	0
Nondisplaced	25.5	36.4	23.6	14.5
Denver				
Displaced	46.9	34.4	15.6	3.1
Nondisplaced	24.5	32.7	26.5	16.3
Richmond				
Displaced	87.5	12.5	0	0
Nondisplaced	60.0	22.0	14.0	4.0
Seattle				
Displaced	37.5	18.8	31.3	12.5
Nondisplaced	23.8	28.8	31.3	16.3
Overall average				
Displaced	48.8	22.6	20.2	8.3
Nondisplaced	34.2	25.8	22.6	17.4

Are Displaced Households Worse Off after Relocation?

On the whole, displaced households do not appear to live in worse conditions following their move. As table 30 shows, a majority of 61 percent of the displaced movers rated their current home as either excellent or good, while 60 percent rated their current neighborhood as either excellent or good. Majorities of 67 percent and 56 percent of the displaced sample also indicated that they liked their current homes and neighborhoods better than their old ones.

An analysis of objective indicators such as rent and crowding indicates that, on the average, displaced households paid about one-fifth more rent for their new homes than they did for their previous ones (see table 31). Median monthly rents increased by $35, from $188 to $223. Even though rents increased, displaced households evidently purchased additional rooms with their higher rental payments, since their ratio of rent per room was the same after the move as before. On the average, however, this increased space did not reduce overall residential density, which remained at a relatively comfortable 0.51 persons per room. That displaced households did not reduce residential density is, no doubt, attributable to increases

Table 30 EVALUATION OF NEW HOMES AND NEIGHBORHOODS
(PERCENTAGES)

TYPE OF MOVER	EXCELLENT	GOOD	FAIR	POOR
	Rating of Current House			
Nondisplaced	27	44	24	5
Displaced	16	45	30	9
Chi square = 8.43	Significance = 0.04[a]			
	Rating of Current Neighborhood			
Nondisplaced	25	45	24	5
Displaced	19	41	31	9
Chi square = 5.19	Significance = 0.15[a]			

	MUCH BETTER	SLIGHTLY BETTER	SAME	SLIGHTLY WORSE	MUCH WORSE
	Comparison of Current Home to Previous One				
Nondisplaced	62	22	9	0	2
Displaced	48	19	17	11	5
Chi square = 14.37	Significance = 0.01[a]				
	Comparison of Current Neighborhood to Previous One[b]				
Nondisplaced	46	21	20	9	4
Displaced	33	23	24	15	4
Chi square = 5.63	Significance = 0.23[a]				

a. The chi-square statistic is used to test the null hypothesis that the numbers appearing in the tables were generated by a completely random process. The alternative hypothesis is that these numbers were generated because of the relationship that exists between these variables. A significance of less than 0.05 is enough to reject the null hypothesis.
b. For those who changed neighborhoods (409 cases).

in household size. Even for households with the same number of members after the move as before, however, the median person-per-room ratio did not change. Finally, displaced households tended to move to locations that reduced the time needed to commute to work. Among those who worked, 22 percent had shorter commutes after being displaced, and only 15 percent traveled longer distances.

Are Displaced Households Worse Off after Moving in Comparison with Nondisplaced Movers?

Even though a majority of displaced households do not seem to be worse off in terms of housing after their move, they appear to fare less well than the sample of voluntary movers. A larger proportion of the voluntary households than of the displaced ones rated their new homes and neighborhoods positively. For example, 71 percent

113

Table 31 CHANGES IN HOUSING CHARACTERISTICS AND COMMUTATION TIMES

	NONDISPLACED MOVERS	DISPLACED MOVERS
Median rent before move	$194	$188
Median rent after move	$253	$223
Percent increase in median rent	30	19
Median rent per room before move	$ 56	$ 56
Median rent per room after move	$ 71	$ 56
Percent increase in median rent per room	27	0
Median persons per room before move	.60	.51
Median persons per room after move	.50	.51
Percent increase in median persons per room	–17	0
Percent household heads with longer commutes following the move	29	15
Percent household heads with shorter commutes following the move	18	22

of nondisplaced movers rated their current house good or excellent, compared with 61 percent of the displaced households. In addition, 70 percent of voluntary movers compared with 60 percent of displaced households rated their current neighborhood positively. Even when the responses of the nondisplaced households are broken down into five categories of movers, the displaced still rate their homes and neighborhoods less positively than any other group of movers.

Similarly, when comparing their current and previous homes and neighborhoods, nondisplaced households responded more positively than their displaced counterparts. Overall, 84 percent of nondisplaced movers said their new homes were better than their old ones, while only 67 percent of displaced households responded this positively. Twice the percentage of displaced households as nondisplaced households indicated that their current homes were worse than their previous ones. Again, when the nondisplaced households are regrouped into five categories, the displaced still respond more negatively than any other group of movers.

This pattern also holds for comparisons of current and previous neighborhoods. Sixty-seven percent of nondisplaced households evaluated their current neighborhoods as better than their previous ones, compared with 56 percent of the displaced households. Nineteen percent of the displaced group said their new neighborhood was worse compared to only 13 percent of the nondisplaced sample.

In order to determine whether the displaced population's assessments of housing and neighborhood conditions were significantly different from the nondisplaced sample's assessments, chi-square tests were used. The tests show that a household's reaction to its new home—both in rating it independently and in comparing it to its previous home—is dependent on whether the household was displaced or whether it moved voluntarily. However, the household's reaction to its new neighborhood does not seem to be significantly influenced by its reason for moving.

Objective indicators are more mixed, however. Voluntary movers had steeper rent increases than displaced households (30 percent rise compared with 19 percent), yet by paying the increased rent the voluntary movers were able to reduce their crowding. For voluntary movers, the person-per-room ratio decreased by 17 percent, while for displaced households the ratio remained constant. Displaced households, however, more frequently had shorter commutes after moving than did nondisplaced outmovers.

Displaced households took longer, on the whole, than voluntary movers to find their new homes. Eighteen percent of the displaced households spent more than six months finding their current homes, while 13 percent of those not displaced took that long. There is some ambiguity about considering the time it took to relocate to be a hardship variable. The longer spans may indicate that the displaced were able to take their time and make a wise and unpressured housing choice. A more probable explanation is that the displaced were forced to live with neighbors and relatives during the search, thus resulting in hardship. Finally, the longer periods may reflect the difficulty experienced in locating affordable and acceptable housing.

Does Displacement Cause a Household To Have Worse Housing?

Is displacement causally related to a household's negative reaction to its new home? The discussion above indicates that whether a household was displaced or not was significantly related to that household's reaction to its new home. To investigate whether displacement was responsible for a negative reaction, however, we need a different type of analysis. We used a probit analysis designed to find those variables that explain why the households interviewed react negatively to their new homes. The dependent variable in the analysis was a reclassification of the households' responses to the question comparing their current home to their previous home. If a household indicated that its current home was slightly or much worse than its previous one, then that household was deemed to be worse off—in terms of housing satisfaction—after moving. Any other response indicated that the household was not worse off. Among the independent variables examined was displacement. The equation presented in table 32 is the final product of the probit analysis. It presents those variables that were significant in explaining why households may feel worse off in their new homes. (For a detailed description of the development of this model, see the appendix to this chapter.)

At no point in the probit analysis did displacement show up as a signficant variable in explaining why households react negatively to their new homes. Three variables seemed to explain why an outmover would consider the new home worse than the previous one: (1) whether the head of the household was unemployed, (2) whether the household had moved five or more times in the past ten years, and (3) whether the number of persons per room increased. If a household head was married, however, he or she would be more likely to respond that the new home was *better* than the old one.

Do Any Subgroups of the Displaced Encounter Unusual Hardship?

Although displaced households, as a group, do not seem to encounter severe hardships as a result of their relocation, it is important to

Table 32 THE WORSE-OFF MODEL FOR ALL HOUSEHOLDS

INDEPENDENT VARIABLES	CONSTANT	MARRY	UNEMP	MOVE5	CROWD	MVTIME[a]
Coefficient estimate	−1.72	−0.33	0.43	0.44	0.60	0.30
T-ratio	(10.23)	(2.27)	(2.33)	(2.63)	(3.62)	(1.55)

a. This variable was included in the final model, because it appeared significant at some points in the analysis and insignificant at others. Thus one cannot be sure of the extent to which it was important in predicting the dependent variable. We do know, however, that it is not as important as those variables that are significant in this model.

116

delve beneath the aggregate statistics to determine whether any subgroup encountered hardship. A probit equation identical to the one described above was therefore run for displaced households only. In this analysis, a household's comparison of its current to its previous home was the dependent variable, and various indicators such as age, race, household composition, and income were the independent variables. The analysis was designed to indicate which characteristics, if any, were causally related to a displaced household's feeling that its current home was worse than its previous one. The final equation of this analysis is presented in table 33. (For a detailed description of the development of this model, see the appendix to this chapter.)

The probit analysis indicates that only two variables were significantly related to whether a displaced household rates its new home worse than its previous one. Those households whose heads were unemployed and those that had moved five or more times in the last ten years were the most likely to feel that their current home was worse than their previous one. Contrary to our expectations, low-income households and the elderly were not more likely to encounter hardship as a result of displacement than other groups.

How Do the Results of the Displacement Study Fit in with the Existing Literature?

As discussed in chapter 3, very little empirical evidence exists to describe the displacement phenomenon and its consequences. Previous studies support certain of the findings described above and conflict with others.

On the question of the characteristics of displaced households, our findings that elderly households have only a slightly greater chance of being displaced and that those households whose heads have less formal education have a significantly greater chance of being displaced

Table 33 WORSE-OFF MODEL FOR DISPLACED HOUSEHOLDS

INDEPENDENT VARIABLES	CONSTANT	UNEMP	MOVE5	EDUC[a]
Coefficient estimate	−2.25	0.79	0.81	0.09
T-ratio	(5.54)	(2.51)	(2.54)	(1.65)

a. See note to table 32.

seem to agree with the findings of most of these studies. Our finding that certain groups of nonwhites have a higher probability of being displaced is also supported by the findings of the NIAS and Annual Housing Survey studies. On the other hand, our findings that lower-income households are significantly more likely to be displaced and that income and displacement are consistently inversely related contradict both the Hayes Valley and the University of Michigan studies, which reported a significant number of higher-income displacees.

The finding that displaced households tend to move to locations near their original neighborhoods is supported by the two studies that have collected data on this question. The NIAS study of displacement in Hayes Valley reports that almost half the households it examined moved to homes in either the same or an adjacent planning district, and a very small proportion (9 percent) moved outside the city. The University of Michigan research also indicates that "movement across jurisdictional boundaries even within the same SMSA is relatively rare."[6]

The somewhat surprising result that displaced households tend to be satisfied with their new homes and neighborhoods is also supported by the results of the other empirical studies. That displaced households are somewhat less positive about their new homes and neighborhoods than the nondisplaced households is consistent with the Seattle but not the Hayes Valley research. The findings that rent increases were for the most part relatively modest and that crowding did not seem to worsen confirm the findings of the four studies discussed in chapter 3.

Discussion

Perhaps the most unexpected and important finding that recurs throughout the empirical displacement literature, including this study, is that the popular image of the displaced outmover is grossly inaccurate. That image is of the outmover as either elderly or part of a nonwhite household (or both), afflicted with ills that range from having to pay unaffordable rents for substandard units to suffering from severe depression.

At the outset of this chapter we offered several hypotheses about the results of the displacement survey. Several of these predictions were supported by the data; a number were not. As expected, the poor and unemployed were especially susceptible to being displaced. Hispanics were also more likely to be displaced, but blacks were not.

Low educational attainment and being elderly surprisingly were not causally related to whether a household would be displaced.

Contrary to our expectations, for the most part, displaced households did not seem to suffer severe hardship as a result of displacement. Most indicated that their new homes were as good as or better than their old ones; rent increases were moderate, and crowding remained constant. Whether or not a household was displaced was found not to cause that household to be dissatisfied with new housing conditions. Even so—as expected—households that moved for reasons other than displacement, on the whole, were more satisfied.

Finally, only two subgroups of the displaced population seemed to encounter disproportionate hardship—the unemployed and the transient. Contrary to our predictions, households that earned low incomes or that were headed by someone over the age of sixty-five, or were in a racial minority were not made especially worse off by displacement.

Being displaced must indeed be unpleasant, even traumatic, yet its effects on the whole do not seem especially burdensome to the displaced. Perhaps the most persuasive explanation for this phenomenon rests with the concept of inertia. For the most part, the neighborhoods from which low-income households have been displaced do not appear to resemble idealized, closely knit, ethnic neighborhoods such as Gans's West End or Cybriwsky's Fairmount. Instead, these neighborhoods are more often the breeding grounds of urban problems. High concentrations of very low-income people, deteriorating housing, and people frightened by rampant crime more often typify these areas. Low-income households continue to live in these neighborhoods not only because of the low-cost housing they contain, but also because many lack the skills and resources to seek out more suitable neighborhoods. Displacement, although certainly not a pleasant experience, may serve as the catalyst for breaking through this inertia. Households are forced by displacement to take action necessary to find alternative accommodations. It appears that in the process of being forced to relocate and find new accommodations, most actually upgrade their conditions, at least in their own estimation.

That most households succeeded in upgrading their housing and neighborhood conditions after displacement seems remarkable to those familiar with urban housing markets. Low vacancy rates and rising rents have shrunk the quantity of low-cost housing, as have disinvestment and abandonment. This depiction of urban housing, however, is simplistic. Indeed, many cities do have very tight housing markets, which hinder the mobility of low-income households and reduce the likelihood of their finding adequate and affordable housing. On the other hand, with the loss of population experienced by most cities as higher-income households fled to suburban and exurban locations in the sixties and seventies, a surplus of housing units has sometimes developed. In most cities there exist neighborhoods with vacancy rates considerably higher than the citywide average in which it is somewhat easier to find low-cost housing.

In part, the finding that displacement did not, on the average, result in severe hardships, even in cities with tight housing markets, can be attributed to the slow pace of the reinvestment and displacement processes. As the data presented in chapter 4 indicate, except for one or two of the neighborhoods, revitalization has been occurring gradually, and population turnover has been relatively slow. There remains in each of the revitalizing neighborhoods a significant number of low-income households. Because massive displacement usually does not occur within a short period, there is no onslaught of low-income households bidding up the price of low-cost housing. In addition, in most cities, revitalizing neighborhoods are matched by areas suffering from the opposite process, thereby creating additional low-cost housing opportunities.

Finally, it is conceivable that much of the attention paid to the displacement issue has had a beneficial effect. Community organizations have often assisted the displaced with moral support and counseling. Developers and investors are attempting, in at least some instances, to provide adequate notice before eviction so that households have more time to locate housing. Some have offered relocation assistance in the form of counseling or monetary compensation. In addition, local governments, still sensitive to the uproar over displacement in the years of massive urban renewal, have assisted uprooted households by advising them of their options and, in some cases, by making housing subsidies available.

Appendix to Chapter 5:
A Probit Model for the Analysis of Displacement

This section presents the technical details on the development and estimation of the probit models presented in chapter 5. The analysis presented here is entirely a probit analysis. The section first discusses the nature of the data used, then describes the probit model and the procedure used to arrive at the final equations. Finally, a few key equations used in making the inferences discussed in chapter 5 are presented.

Construction of the models was complicated by the discontinuous nature of the information contained in the displacement survey. Except for the variables which represent income and education, all of the independent variables used in the probit equations are dichotomous, with a "one" representing the fact that the observed household possessed the given characteristic and a "zero" representing the fact that it did not. Moveover, our dependent variable in every equation is also dichotomous. It would therefore have been inappropriate to estimate the models by the standard ordinary least-squares procedure. Thus we were constrained to use the more complex probit model,[7] and a maximum-likelihood estimation procedure[8] was used to obtain the parameter estimates.

In responding to the question on income in the survey, a household identified a range within which its income fell. In representing income in the models, we chose the midpoint of the range indicated as a proxy for the income of that household. If the household indicated that its income was over $25,000—which was the highest range available on the questionnaire—we used $37,500, the midpoint between $25,000 and $50,000, to represent that household's income. Clearly, this variable does not accurately represent the sampled household's income. However, it should suffice as a proxy. We used the number of years of schooling completed as an index for the level of educational achievement of the head of household.

Income and education were the only variables used in the equations that were not dichotomous. We therefore need to be careful when interpreting the coefficients associated with them. The coefficients reported in the tables are comparable to those of the other variables if we bear the following differences in mind. For INCOME, the coefficient is to be interpreted as the impact on the dependent variable of a $1,000 change in the household's income. For EDUC, the coefficient represents the impact on the dependent variable of an increase by one in the number of years of schooling completed by the head of the household. The other coefficients represent the impact on the dependent variable caused by the possession of the characteristic represented by the associated independent variable.

In representing race, the excluded category was whites, and for the place dummies, the excluded category was Seattle because these were the largest categories in their respective group.

In the models that follow, "worse off" is defined to reflect the observed household's reported dissatisfaction with its new home relative to the one it had occupied while living in one of the neighborhoods included in this study. This information was obtained from question 21 of the survey (see appendix A). A household was deemed to be worse off if it responded that its new home was "slightly worse" or "much worse" than its previous home. Any other response indicated that at worst, the household did not lose anything in housing satisfaction as a result of moving. In the displacement model, the dependent variable, which reflected whether the household was displaced or not, was obtained from question 4 of the survey. If the household indicated that it moved because it could no longer afford the rent, because of eviction, or because the house that it rented was sold, then that household was deemed to have been displaced.

An understanding of the following terms and their definitions will be helpful in understanding the probit models presented:

POV Whether a household is below the poverty level (adjusted for size of household).

INERT Whether a household had lived in one of the neighborhoods for more than ten years.

DISPL Whether a household was displaced or not.

SINGLE Whether a household is a single-person household.

MVTIME Whether a household took six or more months to find its new home.

FEMHD3 Whether a household was female-headed with three or more persons.

CROWD Whether a household was more crowded after the move.

MOVE5 Whether a household moved five or more times in the past ten years.

MARRY Whether the head of house was married or not.

UNEMP Whether the head of house was unemployed or not.

WSEOFF Whether a household suffered some loss in housing satisfaction.

BLACK Whether the head of house was black.

HISPAN Whether the head of house was Hispanic.

WHITE Whether the head of house was white.

RENTUP Whether the household experienced an increase in rent.

SMTOLGE Whether a household moved from a small to a large building.

AGED Whether the head of house was sixty-five years of age or older.

HSIZ Whether the household had more than five persons.

122

HSIZEGT4 Whether the household previously had four or more persons.

RENT1 Whether the household paid less than $125 previously.

RENT2 Whether a household paid between $125 and $250 previously.

APT5 Whether a household lived in a building with more than five apartments.

OTHER Whether the head of a household belonged to a racial group other than whites, blacks, and Hispanics.

INCOME The income of the household (determined as outlined above).

EDUC Number of years of schooling completed.

Also included in the models are dummy variables that represent the fact that an observed household lived in a specific city. These variables include the following cities:

BOST Boston
CIN Cincinnati
DEN Denver
RICH Richmond
SEA Seattle

The probit model assumes that the dependent variable is generated by the following mechanism. It assumes that there exists a normally distributed variable z with a mean of zero and a variance of one. Then, if $X(i)$ represents a vector of characteristics of the i-th household and B is the vector of coefficients, the dependent variable is set to one if $X(i)*B$ is greater than or equal to z; otherwise the dependent variable is set to zero.

Let $f(z)$ represent the standard normal density and $F(z)$ the corresponding cummulative distribution. We then have,

$$Pr\,[y(i) = 1|X(i)*B] = Pr[z\leq = X(i)*B] = F[X(i)*B]$$

and

$$Pr[y(i) = 0|X(i)*B] = 1 - F[X(i)*B]$$

where $y(i)$ represents the value of the dependent variable for the i-th observation. The maximum likelihood estimate of the B's can then be obtained by maximizing the likelihood function, which is the joint probability of obtaining the distribution of the dependent variable appearing in the sample.

Before we present the models, a caveat about how we think about the inferences discussed in chapter 5 is in order. All of the tests used here to check the validity of the hypotheses used during the course of the investigation are based on asymptotic statistical theory. Care and some degree of intuition are needed when making such inferences on the basis of a finite, albeit large, data set. There will be borderline cases in which one cannot be completely certain about what the data are saying. To minimize error, one is inclined to make statements only when the signals coming from the analysis are strong and unequivocal. We will highlight those points in the analysis where some legitimate questions may be raised.

Why use a probit analysis? This is a legitimate question, and there is no easy response. Probits require that the error term be identically, independently, and normally distributed across all observations. Clearly, we cannot guarantee this, and indeed, there are very few empirical studies in any field where all of the fundamental assumptions of the method of analysis used are satisfied. However, to the extent that we have found no reason to suspect that the error terms follow a statistical distribution different from the normal, our use of a probit analysis is not inappropriate. Given the constraints imposed by the nature of the data and the questions in which we are interested, the probit model seems to be the most appropriate analytical tool available. Also, to the extent that our results do not differ dramatically from those of the simpler frequency and contingency table analyses, we feel confident that our inferences are robust.

Chapter 5 showed the final, preferred equations that resulted from the probit analysis. Here we describe the procedure used to arrive at these equations. For each model we started with what we call the "general model." This model included as independent or explanatory variables all of the variables we considered to be important in explaining movements in the dependent variable, and for which we had information from the survey. Our choice of independent variables was based on two criteria. We perused the literature for those variables that were supposedly good predictors of the relevant dependent variable and then extracted from this list those variables for which we had information. The probit equation was then estimated to determine which variables were actually good predictors of the dependent variable.

Having estimated the equations, we inspected the ratio of each parameter estimate to its standard deviation. This ratio was used as a substitute for the standard t-ratio; for convenience, we call this statistic the t-ratio in the following discussion. A coefficient is statistically significant at the 95 percent level of confidence if the t-ratio is greater than 1.96. If a variable had a t-ratio of less than

1.96, we dropped it from the equation, since the small t-ratio indicated that by itself this variable did not add significantly to the power of the model to predict the dependent variable. If more than one variable was dropped, a log likelihood ratio test[9] was conducted to check whether those variables cumulatively contributed anything to the power of the model.

Extra care was taken at this point to check the degree to which exclusion of any seemingly insignificant variable caused perturbations in the parameter estimates of the retained variables and their t-ratios. If drastic changes took place—for example, if a formerly significant variable suddenly became insignificant or if the coefficient estimates fluctuated considerably—the reasons for these changes were thoroughly investigated. In such cases it is unlikely that the excluded variables will show up as insignificant using the log likelihood test. Asymptotically, the log likelihood test and the t-ratio test should give identical signals. However, if there were conflicting signals, the variable or variables that caused the controversy were *not* dropped.

This procedure was repeated until the point was reached where the value of the t-ratio associated with each variable remaining in the model was greater than one. At this point, variables were dropped one at a time in order of ascending t-ratios (only if this ratio was less than 1.96). If two variables were correlated, only the variable with the strongest influence on the dependent variable remained in the equation. Thus we were able to minimize the degree to which any multicollinearity between the variables in the models would inflate the estimates of the standard deviation of the parameters, and therefore improve the value of our inferences.

We can safely say that the inferences that were made using this stepwise procedure are robust given the data. However, we may have understated the effect of some important variables in the process of exclusion, since only the variables with the strongest influence are retained. Suppose, for example, we knew that variables x and y were correlated, and suppose now that variable x showed up in the probit equation as the stronger of the two. Thus, using our criteria for dropping insignificant variables, we would drop y; however, there is no guarantee that if x was excluded and y retained, y would not show up as significant. What may be happening in such a situation is that each variable is proxying for some other variable, say z, for which we do not have information. On the other hand, if x is indeed the actual variable, then our inferences are correct. So, at worst, we will admit one variable, which is proxying for another variable for which we do not have information, and exclude a variable that is possibly another good proxy. Also, if two variables are correlated but show up as significant in an equation, then this certainly attests to the strength of each variable separately in predicting the dependent variable. As best we could, we have attempted through various re-specifications of each model to investigate in exhaustive detail these possibilities and present only those equations that seemed to depict best what the available data were telling us.

For the two models with WSEOFF as the dependent variable (see tables 35 and 36), the dependent variables were grouped in four categories: race, place, inherent, and move-related. There were two reasons for grouping the variables in this manner. First, we expected some collinearity to exist between the variables in each of the latter two categories. For example, POV, AGED, UNEMP, and INERT were some variables in the group of inherent characteristics. It seems clear that there would be some relationship between being unemployed and being below the poverty level, or being a household with its head aged sixty-five years or older and being inert in terms of household mobility. The race and place groups were "natural" variables.

Thinking of these variables in these groups allowed us to eliminate those variables that were weak in the sense that they did not add significantly to the power of the model to predict movements in the dependent variable. In this way we could reduce the complexity of the model and reduce leakage of influences across correlated independent variables and in general improve the quality of the models. Only those variables within a given group, which displayed the strongest influence on the dependent variable, were kept as explanatory variables.

In the displacement model all of the independent variables in some way describe a characteristic of the household before moving. We did not categorize these variables. Variables were eliminated sequentially in the manner described until the preferred model was obtained. (See table 34.)

We now present some of the key equations on the basis of which the inferences of chapter 5 were made. Table 35 represents the model investigating those characteristics which make both voluntary and displaced households feel worse off in terms of housing satisfaction after moving. Table 36 provides the same information for displaced households only. The stages shown are as follows:

1. the general model, which includes all the variables that potentially had some power to explain why households may be worse off;

Table 34 DEVELOPMENT OF DISPLACEMENT MODEL FOR ALL HOUSEHOLDS

INDEPENDENT VARIABLES	GENERAL MODEL	STAGE 1	STAGE 2	STAGE 3	PREFERRED MODEL
Constant	-0.91 (2.75)[a]	-0.80 (2.90)	-0.80 (3.44)	-0.88 (4.09)	-0.99 (4.71)
BOST	-0.16 (0.76)	-0.13 (0.63)	—	—	—
CIN	-0.31 (1.35)	-0.30 (1.33)	-0.22 (1.21)	—	—
DEN	0.15 (0.59)	0.16 (0.63)	—	—	—
RICH	-0.59 (2.13)	-0.55 (2.08)	-0.50 (2.15)	-0.36 (1.63)	—
SEA[b]	—	—	—	—	—
WHITE[b]	—	—	—	—	—
BLACK	0.13 (0.62)	0.14 (0.70)	—	—	—
HISPAN	0.33 (1.11)	0.34 (1.17)	0.49 (1.99)	0.54 (2.28)	0.66 (2.83)
OTHER	-0.36 (1.66)	-0.35 (1.63)	-0.36 (1.83)	-0.27 (1.44)	—
POV	0.12 (0.61)	—	—	—	—
AGED	-0.47 (1.79)	-0.42 (1.76)	-0.45 (1.91)	-0.40 (1.75)	—
HSIZGT4	0.23 (1.14)	0.28 (1.41)	0.26 (1.31)	—	—
MARRY	-0.25 (1.61)	-0.25 (1.62)	-0.24 (1.60)	—	—
UNEMP	0.41 (2.20)	0.43 (2.35)	0.45 (2.53)	0.44 (2.56)	0.35 (2.36)
FEMHD3	0.51 (2.74)	0.50 (2.73)	0.51 (2.77)	0.45 (2.61)	0.40 (2.33)
MOVE5	0.02 (0.12)	—	—	—	—
INCOME[c]	-0.02 (2.44)	-0.03 (3.17)	-0.03 (3.33)	-0.03 (3.77)	-0.03 (3.48)
EDUC	0.008 (0.35)	—	—	—	—
INERT	0.14 (0.72)	—	—	—	—
SINGLE	0.42 (2.47)	0.44 (2.67)	0.43 (2.63)	0.49 (3.24)	0.48 (3.25)
APT5	-0.31 (1.44)	-0.35 (1.55)	-0.30 (1.51)	—	—
RENT1	0.26 (1.23)	0.20 (1.06)	0.20 (1.08)	—	—
RENT2	0.13 (0.84)	—	—	—	—
Memorandum: Percentage predicted correctly	78.9	78.9	80.1	78.9	78.9

127

Table 34 cont'd

N (number of independent variables)	21	16	13	8	5
Log of likelihood function	-238.15	-239.37	-240.44	-245.39	-248.94

a. Figures in parentheses are t-ratios.
b. Reference categories.
c. The coefficient on INCOME represents the effect on the dependent variable of a $1,000 change in the household's income.

2. what happens to the models when race variables are excluded, given that their t-values were less than 1.96;
3. when insignificant variables that represent inherent characteristics of the household are removed;
4. when insignificant place variables are removed, and
5. when insignificant move-related characteristics are dropped.

The log likelihood ratio test was used to check whether the exclusion of the variables significantly reduced the power of the model to predict whether the household was worse off or not. In all cases, the exclusion of variables was acceptable.

Table 35 DEVELOPMENT OF WORSE-OFF MODEL FOR ALL HOUSEHOLDS

INDEPENDENT VARIABLES	GENERAL MODEL	RACE VARIABLES EXCLUDED	INHERENT CHARACTERISTICS EXCLUDED	PLACE VARIABLES EXCLUDED	PREFERRED MODEL
Constant	-2.03	-2.05	-2.00	-2.16	-1.72
	(5.33)a	(5.67)	(6.68)	(8.15)	(10.23)
BOST	-0.41	-0.39	-0.40	—	—
	(1.56)	(1.63)	(1.67)		
CIN	-0.26	-0.24	-0.22	—	—
	(0.97)	(0.97)	(0.90)		
DEN	0.11	0.13	0.10	—	—
	(0.38)	(0.54)	(0.43)		
RICH	-0.76	-0.73	-0.67	—	—
	(1.78)	(1.78)	(1.71)		
SEAb	—	—	—	—	—
WHITEb	—	—	—	—	—
BLACK	0.01	—	—	—	—
	(0.05)				
HISPAN	0.01	—	—	—	—
	(0.02)				
OTHER	-0.06	—	—	—	—
	(0.22)				

128

Table 35 cont'd

POV	-0.11	-0.11	—	—	—
	(0.43)	(0.44)			
AGED	-0.17	-0.18	—	—	—
	(0.57)	(0.60)			
HSIZ	0.38	0.37	—	—	—
	(0.76)	(0.76)			
MARRY	-0.38	-0.39	-0.36	-0.37	-0.33
	(2.00)	(2.01)	(2.05)	(2.13)	(2.27)
UNEMP	0.49	0.50	0.44	0.51	0.43
	(2.12)	(2.24)	(2.21)	(2.59)	(2.33)
FEMHD3	0.05	0.04	—	—	—
	(0.22)	(0.19)			
MOVE5	0.47	0.47	0.48	0.47	0.44
	(2.51)	(2.52)	(2.66)	(2.64)	(2.63)
INCOME	0.01	0.01	0.01	0.01	—
	(1.08)	(1.11)	(1.47)	(1.70)	
EDUC	0.01	0.01	—	—	—
	(0.38)	(0.39)			
INERT	0.37	0.37	0.32	0.15	—
	(1.53)	(1.52)	(1.38)	(0.68)	
DISPL	0.20	0.21	0.21	0.26	—
	(1.03)	(1.06)	(1.08)	(1.38)	
CROWD	0.59	0.59	0.59	0.59	0.60
	(3.45)	(3.44)	(3.51)	(3.52)	(3.62)
SMTOLGE	0.29	0.28	0.26	0.28	—
	(1.55)	(1.54)	(1.44)	(1.60)	
MVTIME	0.40	0.40	0.39	0.33	0.30
	(1.92)	(1.96)	(1.91)	(1.66)	(1.55)
Memorandum:					
Percentage predicted correctly	89.9	89.9	89.8	89.9	89.4
N (number of independent variables)	21	18	13	9	5
Log of the likelihood function	-143.62	-143.65	-144.23	-147.60	-151.23

a. Figures in parentheses are t-ratios.
b. Original reference categories.
c. The coefficient on INCOME represents the effect on the dependent variable of a $1,000 change in the household's income.

129

Table 36 DEVELOPMENT OF WORSE-OFF MODEL FOR DISPLACED HOUSEHOLDS

INDEPENDENT VARIABLES	GENERAL MODEL	INHERENT CHARACTERISTICS EXCLUDED	RACE VARIABLES EXCLUDED	MOVE-RELATED VARIABLES EXCLUDED	PREFERRED MODEL
Constant	-1.90	-1.73	-2.02	-1.90	-2.25
	(2.18)[a]	(2.99)	(4.07)	(4.17)	(5.54)
BOST	-1.02	-1.05	-0.77	-0.79	—
	(1.64)	(1.84)	(1.53)	(1.61)	
CIN	-0.89	-0.96	-1.03	-1.08	—
	(1.38)	(1.53)	(1.80)	(1.91)	
DEN	-0.88	-0.97	-0.66	-0.64	—
	(1.39)	(1.62)	(1.57)	(1.58)	
RICH	-0.93	-0.85	-0.78	-0.65	—
	(0.97)	(1.06)	(1.00)	(0.87)	
SEA[b]	—	—	—	—	—
WHITE[b]	—	—	—	—	—
BLACK	-0.33	-0.49	—	—	—
	(0.50)	(0.82)			
HISPAN	0.31	0.10	—	—	—
	(0.45)	(0.16)			
OTHER	-0.58	-0.52	—	—	—
	(0.77)	(0.77)			
POV	-0.51	—	—	—	—
	(0.94)				
AGED	-0.07	—	—	—	—
	(0.11)				
MARRY	-0.30	—	—	—	—
	(0.75)				
UNEMP	1.01	0.91	0.85	0.81	0.79
	(2.02)	(2.30)	(2.43)	(2.42)	(2.51)
FEMHD3	0.21	—	—	—	—
	(0.42)				
MOVE5	0.73	0.62	0.69	0.73	0.81
	(1.70)	(1.67)	(1.95)	(2.16)	(2.54)
INCOME[c]	0.01	—	—	—	—
	(0.08)				
EDUC	0.12	0.12	0.12	0.12	0.09
	(1.89)	(1.98)	(2.05)	(2.01)	(1.65)
INERT	0.24	—	—	—	—
	(0.39)				
CROWD	0.23	0.20	0.27	—	—
	(0.59)	(0.55)	(0.75)		
SMTOLGE	0.18	0.16	0.10	—	—
	(0.42)	(0.39)	(0.28)		
MVTIME	-0.23	-0.17	-0.14	—	—
	(0.44)	(0.35)	(0.30)		
Memorandum:					
Percentage predicted correctly	85.4	84.5	85.3	85.4	83.6
N (number of independent variables)	19	13	10	7	3

Table 36 cont'd

Log of likelihood function	-36.81	-37.92	-38.49	-38.91	-41.56

a. Figures in parentheses are t-ratios.
b. Original reference categories.
c. The coefficient on INCOME represents the effect on the dependent variable of a change of $1,000 in the household's income.

CHAPTER 6

Neighborhood Reinvestment, Displacement, and Public Policy

The most important issue in discussions and debates about displacement at both the national and local levels is whether neighborhood reinvestment should be encouraged or whether it should be slowed down out of concern for the problems it creates for those who are displaced. From our vantage point of a special concern for the condition and prospects of large, older cities in the nation, we feel that the benefits of neighborhood reinvestment, assessed in chapter 2, outweigh the human costs indicated by our research findings.

The problem of displacement is difficult to analyze; moreover, the subject is an emotional one. Others who review the findings presented in chapter 5 may conclude that the problem is more serious than we have judged it to be. Despite a displacement rate of 23 percent for all movers in the nine areas studied, only one in six among those displaced felt that their housing condition had deteriorated. We do not conclude that a policy of benign neglect is the answer to the problems created by displacement; on the contrary, public policies and programs should assist persons who are displaced. Our conclusion that the problem of displacement has not reached a level that would justify public efforts to prevent private reinvestment in inner-city neighborhoods reflects conditions we observed in 1980. Changing economic conditions may bring about an increase in the rate of displacement in the future. Further tightening of urban housing markets may restrict mobility and make it more difficult for those displaced by neighborhood reinvestment to locate alternative homes.

The Federal Response to Displacement

On the whole, the federal government has taken an ambivalent attitude toward neighborhood reinvestment and displacement. In June 1977, Sen. William Proxmire's Committee on Banking, Housing, and Urban Affairs heard testimony on the displacement issue from a wide range of government officials and neighborhood organizers, and in 1978 Congress passed legislation designed to minimize displacement.

Among the provisions contained in the Housing and Community Development Amendments of 1978 was a requirement that low- and moderate-income people who face displacement be given priority in receiving section 312 housing rehabilitation loans. Congress directed the secretary of the Department of Housing and Urban Development to "review and analyze" the impact of urban development action grants (UDAGs) on low- and moderate-income residential neighborhoods. Congress also directed HUD to study the problem of displacement and report to Congress with "recommendations for the formulation of a national policy to minimize involuntary displacement . . . both publicly and privately financed." The act stated a position on displacement: "The Congress declares that in the administration of federal housing and community development programs, consistent with other program goals and objectives, involuntary displacement of persons from their homes and neighborhoods should be minimized."[1]

The qualification that displacement should be minimized "consistent with other program goals and objectives" indicates what a former assistant secretary of HUD called the "schizophrenic" nature of government policy in this area.[2] For many years, HUD has attempted to stimulate urban revitalization, yet efforts to minimize displacement could, in fact, hold back or reduce the level and rate of neighborhood reinvestment. Robert Embry, assistant secretary of HUD under President Carter, expressed departmental policy on reinvestment and displacement before the Proxmire committee as follows: "The reinvestment phenomenon is a small, hopeful trend that should be encouraged, but . . . public policy must be adjusted to accommodate the needs of those threatened by displacement."[3]

In its 1979 report on displacement, HUD stated:

The most appropriate national policy . . . is for the federal government to ensure:
• that the displacement of persons in connection with federal or federally assisted programs is minimized;

- where such displacement is unavoidable, that appropriate relocation assistance is provided;

- that efforts are made to expand the housing supply available to low and moderate income persons; and

- that sufficient research and technical assistance is provided to encourage and support the efforts of state and local governments, neighborhood-based groups, and the private sector to enable them to develop appropriate strategies and activities to minimize displacement and any attending hardships caused by private revitalization.[4]

Therefore, the federal government in the late seventies accepted responsibility for displacement resulting from HUD programs and urged that this dislocation be minimized. The department has required cities to minimize displacement and to specify in their applications for community development block grants what they plan to do to achieve this objective. This requirement, however, has not been strictly enforced.

An effort by HUD in 1979, toward the end of the Carter administration, to require cities to place more emphasis on devising antidisplacement strategies illustrates the uneasiness of federal officials in regard to the displacement issue. In 1979 the department issued a statement requiring cities to show which of their community development activities would entail displacement and what steps they would take to provide those who had to move with acceptable housing. The announcement said that HUD would consider "plainly inappropriate" any strategy that failed to provide adequate housing to households displaced.[5] Sanctions were announced to enforce implementation of this requirement. There were vociferous protests to the announcement of this new policy in 1979, mostly from city officials. Two years later, in May 1981, the Reagan administration quietly revoked the requirement, as part of its overall effort to reduce regulations.[6]

As for privately induced displacement, HUD's stance has always been that cities can best determine if there is a problem that warrants public action. HUD has conducted research and in some cases provided resources to households that have been displaced by neighborhood revitalization through such programs as section 8 rental supplements, section 312 rehabilitation funds, and section 235 homeownership subsidies. In addition, the department, under the Carter administration, funded twelve "innovative" projects to prevent displacement in revitalizing communities. William Witte observed in 1979 that this federal displacement policy had been piecemeal.

> This approach reflects, however, less a conscious set of decisions by HUD than a felt inability to marshal existing federal legislation and program resources to reconcile objectives of encouraging reinvestment while minimizing displacement. This approach also reflects some significant divisions within the department on the appropriate role the federal government should be playing, in what some believe is an inherently local problem.[7]

More recently, wide-ranging budget reductions in domestic programs put into effect by the Reagan administration, and its overall efforts to deregulate, have brought about a more conservative stance on urban issues. This shift is likely to cause the federal government to reduce its role in influencing local development patterns and public policies relating to neighborhood reinvestment.[8]

The Local Response to Displacement

HUD's actions in the Carter period reflected the views of a faction within HUD that advocated local instead of federal action to deal with the problem of displacement caused by neighborhood reinvestment. The brief sally, late in 1979, to temper this policy by providing for greater federal oversight, however, did not succeed. The second HUD report stated, "Local governments are in the best position to recognize the complexity of a displacement problem within their housing markets and to devise antidisplacement strategies."[9] The agency over time has taken this general position, despite the questionable merits of relying on city governments to minimize displacement. Because gentrification results in the replacement of low-income residents by taxpaying residents, local officials may have an incentive to encourage (or at least not discourage) reinvestment that results in displacement. According to a participant in a HUD-sponsored forum on displacement, "A lot of cities are actively promoting gentrification because they feel the need to raise their tax base."[10] Community groups in such cities as Philadelphia and San Francisco have accused city officials of fostering displacement by encouraging neighborhood reinvestment.[11]

Such policies, however, are by no means universal. Some local governments, apparently realizing that displacement can be an explosive political issue if nothing is done about it, have taken remedial action. In some instances, local officials have been motivated by a fear that their political power bases will erode as low-income households are replaced by those with higher incomes. For whatever motives, many city governments have taken steps either to reduce displacement or to mitigate what are regarded as its ill effects. Washington, D.C., Philadelphia, and New York have enacted laws restricting condominium conversions. In the District of Columbia, for example, owners of apartment buildings in which rents are in the low or medium range cannot convert them to condominiums when the citywide vacancy rate is below 3 percent, unless they obtain the consent of a majority of the tenants.

Washington, D.C., has also used two other regulatory devices to prevent or mitigate displacement. A rent control law not only limits rent increases, but also assures evicted tenants a period during which they can remain in their old apartments while they search for new housing. The law also provides for relocation assistance and gives a tenant the right to purchase the single-family home he or she was renting before the owner may sell to another buyer.[12] The District of Columbia also has an antispeculation law designed to prevent the practice of "flipping." The ordinance levies a capital gains tax on unrenovated residential real estate; the tax rate increases with the amount of capital gains and the shortness of the holding period.

A more common device to help homeowners meet rising property taxes is called a "circuit breaker." Baltimore and Washington, D.C., as well as the states of New York and Pennsylvania provide assistance to low-income households, especially the elderly, in paying property taxes. One purpose is to help owner-occupants stay in their homes despite increases in assessments.[13] In several cities, such as St. Louis and New York, tax relief is also provided as a subsidy to owners who rehabilitate residential buildings to bring them up to code standards. In New York City, the owner receives a tax reduction for up to twelve years; in St. Louis, properties are taxed at preimprovement levels for ten years and then at half of the improved value for the next fifteen years.[14]

A number of cities have also used community development block grant funds to pay for programs designed to prevent displacement and provide relocation assistance. The most popular tool is the subsidized rehabilitation loan. In Boston, Portland (Oregon), Seattle, New York, and Chicago, local governments make low-interest loans available to owner-occupants who renovate their homes to meet code requirements. Community development funds also have been used to provide counseling and relocation assistance.[15] In some jurisdictions, low-income tenant cooperatives can be formed as an antidisplacement tool, using community development money along with other federal and local resources. For example, tenants in a Maryland neighborhood threatened by displacement received community development-funded technical assistance and bought more than four hundred units with federal mortgage insurance.[16] Similar cooperative conversions have taken place in the District of Columbia and New York City.

Policy Conclusions

We shall conclude by outlining the types of policy options available to localities for stimulating reinvestment, minimizing displacement, and preserving and increasing the supply of low-cost housing. It must be emphasized that, while it is important to generalize about the costs and consequences of neighborhood reinvestment, cities differ. A mixture of policies is needed to fit the housing market, fiscal constraints, and political realities of any particular city.

Encouraging Neighborhood Revitalization

The revitalization of inner-city neighborhoods should be welcomed rather than discouraged. Research findings and data presented in chapter 2 demonstrate that, in addition to the rehabilitation of housing, neighborhood reinvestment also results in increases in local tax revenues. Although cities do not necessarily derive increased revenues proportionate to the increased market values of their housing stock, revitalized neighborhoods do generate greater tax revenue than they would have if no renovation had occurred. Though one cannot generalize about how cities will spend this additional money, it is reasonable to expect that most residents will benefit to some degree, either through augmented public services or as a result of the city's improved fiscal position.

As a general rule, cities and the people living in them benefit from the presence of stable households. An increase in relatively high-income households tends to aid the community, both economically and psychologically. Long-time owner-occupants affected by decreasing property values in their neighborhood, deterioration, and increased crime—or the fear of increased crime—are the most likely beneficiaries, if they are able to remain in the neighborhood.

City officials are in a difficult position politically on development and reinvestment issues in older neighborhoods. Fear on the part of residents that they will be displaced may make it impractical for city officials to promote neighborhood reinvestment, even though the public sector has tools to stimulate and facilitate the development process. Among the possible tactics are:

1. Subsidizing the renovation of housing in target neighborhoods through tax abatements, low-interest loans, and grants.
2. Undertaking site improvements including widening, paving, and lighting streets, and sprucing up parks.
3. Encouraging the provision of amenities such as cultural attractions, restaurants, and retail stores.
4. Improving public services, especially crime protection and public education.

Dealing with Displacement

While the results of the displacement survey presented in chapter 5 and the findings of other researchers indicate that most displaced households do not suffer hardship as a result of displacement, it is our judgment that measures should be taken at the local level to assist households that do encounter difficulties.

Moreover, in many cities displacement has become a political issue among those who seek ways to alleviate social problems, but who disagree on the way to do so. On a more general basis, the issue can produce intense controversy between those who believe in neighborhood integration to reduce racial concentration in ghetto areas and those who believe that the real motive for a dispersal or integration approach is to facilitate gentrification and economic development. Such disputes can divert energy from measures to assist low-income households and threaten the existence of political coalitions that have worked in the past to increase the low-income housing stock and improve the conditions of distressed urban neighborhoods.

The balance to be struck is not an easy one. In their efforts to minimize displacement and hardship, city officials risk cutting off the reinvestment process. Some localities have enacted local regulatory devices, such as rent control ordinances and condominium conversion moratoria, in an effort to prevent households from being displaced. Controversy often arises about the effects of these actions. One of the harshest critics of rent control is George Sternlieb, who believes that rent control distorts and undermines the rental market and results in reduced tax valuations, undermaintenance, reduction in new construction, the conversion of rental units to condominiums, and in some cases, abandonment.[17] Defenders of rent control, such as John Gilderbloom, respond by attacking the research on which Sternlieb's conclusions are based. Gilderbloom concludes that "short term, moderate rent controls had little or no impact on the amount of construction, maintenance, or taxable valuation of rental properties."[18]

Regardless of whether or not rent control inevitably harms the persons it is designed to help by narrowing low-income housing opportunities, it probably does slow neighborhood revitalization. In its early stages, reinvestment is a fragile process that tends to build up gradually. Rent control ordinances reduce the likelihood that investors will purchase and restore buildings, since they fear they will be unable to earn a sufficient return. Condominium conversion restrictions can also slow reinvestment by closing off a form of ownership that frequently accompanies revitalization. We conclude that, in trying to minimize displacement, cities as a general rule should not enact restrictive rent control or conversion regulations.

There are, however, positive, although more costly, steps that cities can take to minimize displacement in revitalizing neighborhoods:

1. Enacting "first right of refusal' ordinances allowing tenants the right to purchase any unit they live in that is to be converted to condominiums.
2. Helping low-income households purchase their own homes, either by providing subsidized mortgages or by forming low-income, limited-equity cooperatives.
3. Preventing rising property taxes from displacing low-income owner-occupants by providing tax abatements.
4. Making available inexpensive rehabilitation loans or grants to low-income households to enable them to bring their housing up to code standards.

Despite any efforts to minimize displacement due to neighborhood reinvestment, some low-income residents inevitably will be forced to move. Even though our results indicate that the average household will find satisfactory housing for only a moderate increase in rent, some displaced individuals will need assistance. Cities have several avenues of help for these households. Some of these policies may be costly, especially to cities already strapped for revenue. We feel, however, that since reinvestment brings increased tax revenues for municipalities, they are under an obligation to spend some of these funds to assist those who bear the costs of the process. Among the possible government actions to assist the displaced are:

1. Requiring landlords to give tenants uniform and adequate notice before eviction in order to give them time to find new housing.
2. Advising low-income households on the types of housing available by setting up neighborhood technical assistance units or a city relocation office.
3. Providing temporary rent subsidies or apartments in conventional public housing to displaced tenants.

Preserving and Augmenting the Supply of Low-Cost Housing

Revitalization entails the filtering upward to higher-income use of a housing unit occupied by lower-income households. Unless additional housing is added to the city's low-cost housing stock, the number of units available to lower-income households will decline. Since in many cities the supply of housing available to lower-income households is already low, revitalization will aggravate already-tight housing markets. Where this occurs, the public sector should devise methods to preserve and augment the supply of low-income housing. Although the costs are appreciable—and this is a point that must be emphasized in the current period of retrenchment affecting national urban programs[19]—there are some strategies available:

1. Increasing the supply of low-income housing by building more subsidized units either directly (conventional public housing) or by subsidizing the private sector (section 8 new construction program).
2. Increasing the ability of tenants to afford market-level rents by providing rent supplements.
3. Helping tenants to become owners either of single-family homes or of lower-income, limited-equity cooperatives by renovating city-owned abandoned buildings and selling them for nominal prices.

As we have already noted, local strategies to provide affordable housing to low-income households have to be flexible, depending on

141

the condition of the housing market. Cities with strong markets and very low vacancy rates will need to construct more low-income housing units; increasing demand by providing rent supplements in such cases only leads to further tightening and hardship in the housing market. On the other hand, cities with a weak housing market and many vacancies should avoid increasing the supply of housing, since increasing the surplus can lead to further disinvestment. In these housing markets, stimulating demand and renovating abandoned, but potentially occupiable, buildings would be more appropriate.

All of the available policy options must be considered in the context of economic conditions and trends. Should high interest rates and the resulting slowdown of new housing construction continue through the 1980s, the problem of displacement could become more serious. The demographic and social trends forecast for the next decade, including an increase in households composed of relatively young persons, will increase demand and may fuel reinvestment in the existing housing stock as an alternative to the construction of new homes. Households prevented from purchasing existing homes due to rising prices may be forced to become tenants, producing increased demand and higher rents for existing housing units. Such developments would undoubtedly increase the amount of displacement, and those affected would encounter greater difficulties in locating adequate and affordable homes.

City officials are often placed in a very difficult position by displacement due to neighborhood reinvestment. We would be remiss if we did not lay out and clearly identify our conclusions, but readers may come to different conclusions. We believe that the negative effects of neighborhood reinvestment, specifically displacement, do not outweigh the benefits. As a general rule, we conclude that urban reinvestment in older and declining cities should be encouraged by the public sector, rather than stifled by restrictive measures such as rent control or condominium conversion restrictions. We believe the better course of action to deal with displacement—under the conditions that prevailed when our research was done—is for public policy to concentrate on positive measures to reduce barriers to mobility, particularly efforts to maintain an adequate supply of low-cost housing.

APPENDIX A

Survey Questionnaire and Cover Letter

Princeton University NATIONAL MOVERS SURVEY
PRINCETON URBAN AND REGIONAL RE-
SEARCH CENTER
WOODROW SCHOOL OF PUBLIC AFFAIRS
PRINCETON, NEW JERSEY 08544

January 15, 1981

Dear

Each year one out of five households moves from one home to another, yet no one really knows why so many households move or if they are satisfied with their new residences. We at the Princeton Urban and Regional Research Center are conducting a survey to learn more about why people move and the conditions they face in their new homes.

Your household is one of a few whose opinions we seek on these matters. Your name has been chosen from a list of those who moved from a home in the Mulberry-Vine-Sycamore Streets area sometime during the last year. To make sure that the results of this research truly reflect the views of people who have recently moved from the Mulberry-Vine-Sycamore Streets area, we need you to promptly fill out and return the questionnaire.

It should take you no more than 10 or 15 minutes to complete. When you are finished, please mail it back to us in the enclosed stamped envelope.

If you include the enclosed blue card with the completed questionnaire, we will immediately send you a $5.00 check as our thanks. If you wish to receive the results of our study, please check the box on the blue card.

We will not tell anyone about your answers. The questionnaire has an identification number for mailing purposes only. This is so we may check your name off the mailing list when your questionnaire is returned. Your name will never be placed on the questionnaire.

I would be most happy to answer any questions you might have. Please write or call. My telephone number is (609) 452-5663.

Thank you for your help.

Sincerely yours,

Michael H. Schill
Director

144

INSTRUCTIONS

PLEASE CIRCLE ONLY ONE RESPONSE FOR EACH
QUESTION. YOUR ANSWERS SHOULD ACCURATELY
DESCRIBE YOUR OPINIONS AND HOUSEHOLD
CHARACTERISTICS. WHEN YOU ARE DONE PLEASE
MAIL THE QUESTIONNAIRE AND BLUE CARD IN THE
ENCLOSED REPLY ENVELOPE. DO NOT PUT YOUR
NAME ON THE QUESTIONNAIRE, BUT DO PUT YOUR
NAME AND ADDRESS ON THE BLUE CARD. WHEN WE
GET YOUR BLUE CARD ALONG WITH A FILLED-OUT
QUESTIONNAIRE, WE WILL SEND YOU A CHECK FOR
FIVE DOLLARS AS OUR THANKS FOR YOUR
COOPERATION.

1. How would you rate your current *neighborhood* as a
   place to live—would you say it is excellent, good,
   fair, or poor? (Circle one).

   1. EXCELLENT
   2. GOOD
   3. FAIR
   4. POOR
   5. DON'T KNOW

2. How would you rate your current *house* as a place to
   live—would you say it is excellent, good, fair,
   or poor? (Circle one).

   1. EXCELLENT
   2. GOOD
   3. FAIR
   4. POOR
   5. DON'T KNOW

3. How long had you lived in the Mulberry-Vine-Sycamore
   Streets area before you moved to your current
   address? (Circle correct response).

   1. LESS THAN 1 YEAR
   2. 1-2 YEARS
   3. 3-5 YEARS
   4. 6-10 YEARS

5. OVER 10 YEARS
6. DON'T KNOW

4. What is the main reason why you moved from the home
   in the Mulberry-Vine-Sycamore Streets area that you
   lived in 1979–1980? (Circle only one reason; if no
   response listed below fits your reason for moving,
   please write why you moved in the space marked
   "other").

   1. TRANSFERRED TO A NEW JOB
   2. RETIRED
   3. WANTED TO LIVE CLOSER TO WHERE I WORK
   4. TO ATTEND SCHOOL
   5. RENT INCREASED TOO MUCH
   6. EVICTED BY LANDLORD BECAUSE HOUSE HAD TO
       BE FIXED UP
   7. HOUSE WAS SOLD BY LANDLORD
   8. PROPERTY TAXES INCREASED TOO MUCH
   9. NEEDED LARGER HOUSE OR APARTMENT
   10. NEEDED SMALLER HOUSE OR APARTMENT
   11. CHANGE IN MARITAL STATUS (i.e. RECENTLY MAR-
        RIED, DIVORCED, SEPARATED, OR WIDOWED)
   12. TO LIVE CLOSER TO RELATIVES
   13. WANTED TO ESTABLISH OWN HOUSEHOLD
   14. WANTED BETTER NEIGHBORHOOD
   15. WANTED TO OWN A HOME
   16. WANTED BETTER HOUSE
   17. WANTED BETTER SCHOOLS
   18. WANTED TO RENT A HOME/APARTMENT
   19. NATURAL DISASTER (i.e. HOUSE BURNED DOWN)
   20. OTHER:_____

5. From the day you decided to move, how long did it
   take you to find your current home?

   1. LESS THAN 2 WEEKS
   2. 2–4 WEEKS
   3. 1–3 MONTHS
   4. 4–6 MONTHS
   5. OVER 6 MONTHS
   6. DON'T REMEMBER

6. Did you live in any other homes between the time you left the home in the Mulberry-Vine-Sycamore Streets area that you lived in 1979–1980 and your current home?

   1. YES
   2. NO ⸺⸺⸺⸺⸺⸺⸺ If you haven't lived in any other homes please go to question 8.
   3. DON'T KNOW

7. How many different homes have you lived in since you moved from the house in the Mulberry-Vine-Sycamore Streets area that you lived in 1979–1980?

   1. ONE   4. FOUR
   2. TWO   5. FIVE
   3. THREE   6. SIX

8. How many times have you moved in the past ten years?

   1. ONE TIME   4. FOUR TIMES
   2. TWO TIMES   5. FIVE TIMES
   3. THREE TIMES   6. OVER FIVE TIMES
                      7. DON'T KNOW

Now, some questions about your current home.

9. Do you currently rent or own your home?

   1. RENT
   2. OWN ⸺⸺⸺⸺⸺⸺⸺ If you own your current home please go to question 11.
   3. OTHER
   4. DON'T KNOW

10. (If you rent) How much is your monthly rent, including utilities?

    1. LESS THAN $70   6. $175–199
    2. $70–99   7. $200–249
    3. $100–124   8. $250–274
    4. $125–149   9. $275–299
    5. $150–174   10. $300 OR MORE
                       11. DON'T KNOW

11. How many rooms (excluding bathrooms) are there in

your current home?

1. ONE	7. SEVEN
2. TWO	8. EIGHT
3. THREE	9. NINE
4. FOUR	10. TEN
5. FIVE	11. ELEVEN
6. SIX	12. DON'T KNOW

12. In your current home, on the average, how long does it take for the head of the household to get to work?

1. UNDER 15 MINUTES
2. 15–29 MINUTES
3. 30–44 MINUTES
4. 45–59 MINUTES
5. 1 HOUR TO 1 HOUR 29 MINUTES
6. 1 HOUR & 30 MINUTES OR MORE
7. DON'T KNOW

13. How many other apartments are there in your current building?

1. NONE, IT'S A SINGLE FAMILY HOUSE
2. ONE
3. TWO TO FOUR
4. FIVE TO NINETEEN
5. TWENTY OR MORE
6. DON'T KNOW

14. How many people live in your household?

1. ONE	2. TWO
3. THREE	4. FOUR
5. FIVE	6. SIX
7. SEVEN	8. EIGHT
9. NINE	10. TEN
11. ELEVEN	12. TWELVE
13. THIRTEEN	14. FOURTEEN
15. FIFTEEN	16. SIXTEEN
17. DON'T KNOW	

Now some questions about the home in the Mulberry-Vine-Sycamore Streets area that you used to live in in 1979–1980.

148

15. When you lived in that home in the Mulberry-Vine-Sycamore Streets area, did you rent or own your home?

    1. RENTED
    2. OWNED————————— | If you owned your home please go to question 17.
    3. OTHER
    4. DON'T KNOW

16. (If you used to rent) How much was your monthly rent, including utilities, when you lived in that home in the Mulberry-Vine-Sycamore Streets area?

    1. LESS THAN $70   6. $175–199
    2. $70–99   7. $200–249
    3. $100–124   8. $250–274
    4. $125–149   9. $275–279
    5. $150–174   10. $300 OR MORE
                           11. DON'T KNOW

17. How many rooms were there (excluding bathrooms) in that home in the Mulberry-Vine-Sycamore Streets area that you used to live in?

    1. ONE   7. SEVEN
    2. TWO   8. EIGHT
    3. THREE   9. NINE
    4. FOUR   10. TEN
    5. FIVE   11. ELEVEN
    6. SIX   12. DON'T KNOW

18. When you lived in that home in the Mulberry-Vine-Sycamore Streets area, on the average, how long did it take the head of the household to get to work?

    1. UNDER 15 MINUTES
    2. 15–29 MINUTES
    3. 30–44 MINUTES
    4. 45–59 MINUTES
    5. 1 HOUR TO 1 HOUR 29 MINUTES

6. 1 HOUR & 30 MINUTES OR MORE
7. DON'T KNOW

19. How many other apartments were there in that building in the Mulberry-Vine-Sycamore Streets area?

1. NONE, IT WAS A SINGLE FAMILY HOUSE
2. ONE
3. TWO–FOUR
4. FIVE–NINETEEN
5. TWENTY OR MORE
6. DON'T KNOW

20. When you lived in that home in the Mulberry-Vine-Sycamore Streets area how many people were there living in your household?

1. ONE	2. TWO
3. THREE	4. FOUR
5. FIVE	6. SIX
7. SEVEN	8. EIGHT
9. NINE	10. TEN
11. ELEVEN	12. TWELVE
13. THIRTEEN	14. FOURTEEN
15. FIFTEEN	16. SIXTEEN
	17. DON'T KNOW

21. Compared with your old home in the Mulberry-Vine-Sycamore Streets area would you say you like your current home—

1. MUCH BETTER
2. SLIGHTLY BETTER
3. SAME
4. SLIGHTLY WORSE
5. MUCH WORSE
6. DON'T KNOW

22. Compared with your old neighborhood in the Mulberry-Vine-Sycamore Streets area, would you say you like your current neighborhood—

0. DOESN'T APPLY—I STILL LIVE IN THE MULBERRY-VINE-SYCAMORE STREETS AREA
1. MUCH BETTER

2. SLIGHTLY BETTER
3. SAME
4. SLIGHTLY WORSE
5. MUCH WORSE
6. DON'T KNOW

Finally, a few questions about you and your family.

23. Are you married?

    1. YES
    2. NO

24. What is the sex of the head of your household?

    1. MALE
    2. FEMALE

25. What is the race of the head of your household?

    1. BLACK
    2. HISPANIC
    3. WHITE
    4. ASIAN
    5. AMERICAN INDIAN
    6. OTHER: _____

26. How old is the head of the household?

    1. UNDER 25 YEARS
    2. 25-29 YEARS
    3. 30-34 YEARS
    4. 35-44 YEARS
    5. 45-64 YEARS
    6. 65 YEARS OR OLDER
    7. DON'T KNOW

27. Is the head of the household employed, unemployed,
    or retired? (Circle one)

    1. EMPLOYED
    2. UNEMPLOYED
    3. RETIRED

4. STUDENT
5. OTHER

28. What was the highest grade in school completed by the household head?

0. NEVER ATTENDED SCHOOL
1. KINDERGARTEN
2. FIRST GRADE
3. SECOND GRADE
4. THIRD GRADE
5. FOURTH GRADE
6. FIFTH GRADE
7. SIXTH GRADE
8. SEVENTH GRADE
9. EIGHTH GRADE
10. NINTH GRADE
11. TENTH GRADE
12. ELEVENTH GRADE
13. TWELFTH GRADE
14. 1ST YEAR COLLEGE
15. 2ND YEAR COLLEGE
16. 3RD YEAR COLLEGE
17. 4TH YEAR COLLEGE
18. GRADUATE SCHOOL
19. DON'T KNOW

29. Please estimate your household's total yearly income last year (before taxes).

1. 0-$2,999
2. $3,000-4,999
3. $5,000-6,999
4. $7,000-9,999
5. $10,000-14,999
6. $15,000-19,999
7. $20,000-24,999
8. OVER $24,999
9. DON'T KNOW

Thank you very much for your help. Please check through the questionnaire to make sure that you answered all questions completely.

APPENDIX B

A Note on Nonresponse Bias

The sample of households may be biased in two ways. This appendix examines what effect, if any, these possible biases could have on the study's results.

Income

Households at both ends of the income scale could be undersampled. Since movers with low incomes may move in with friends or relatives to economize on rent, we may not have been able to identify and locate them. In addition, some households may not have been able to afford telephones, which provide one of our chief methods of locating households. Households at higher-income levels who have unlisted telephone numbers or moved out of the state were probably also undersampled. With a greater proportion of the displaced sample earning low incomes, if these lower-income displacees tend to be worse off in terms of housing satisfaction than are those who earn higher incomes, then the negative aspects of displacement in the aggregate may be understated. Table B-1, however, fails to show a consistent relationship between income and satisfaction among displaced households. Therefore, even if the lowest-income households were undersampled, it would probably not lead to any understatement of dissatisfaction with housing.

Transience

Another possible source of bias in the sample would be not finding the most transient households, both because they might not be

Table B-1 COMPARISON OF CURRENT AND PREVIOUS HOMES

INCOME LEVEL	CURRENT HOME WORSE THAN PREVIOUS		CURRENT HOME BETTER THAN PREVIOUS	
	NONDISPLACED (PERCENT)	DISPLACED (PERCENT)	NONDISPLACED (PERCENT)	DISPLACED (PERCENT)
0–$4,999	6	23	85	62
$ 5,000–$ 9,999	7	17	85	63
$10,000–$14,999	6	12	82	72
$15,000–$19,999	2	9	92	82
$20,000–$24,999	10	22	88	67
$25,000+	12	17	83	83

Source: Survey results.

included in the R. L. Polk & Company enumeration in the first place, and because their frequent moves would make them harder to find. Although the question of whether the Polk Company systematically misses transient households cannot be examined here, we can get some indication of whether our difficulty in finding these transient households disproportionately affected the displaced sample. If the displacement rate among transient households is greater than the rate for the whole sample, then our undersampling of this population would lead to an understatement of the aggregate displacement rate. However, it appears that among the most transient households in the survey, those who moved five or more times in the past ten years, the displacement rate was only slightly greater than the overall displacement rate for the whole sample.

A potentially more troublesome problem would occur if transient households were especially negatively affected by displacement. The analysis presented in the appendix to chapter 5 indicates that this appears to be so. One of the two factors that are significantly related to a displaced household's relative dissatisfaction with its current home is having moved five or more times in the last ten years. Even though this undersampling may tend to understate the negative aspects of displacement to some small degree, overall even transient households seem satisfied with their new homes: 72 percent of those households that were displaced and moved five or more times in the last ten years reported that their current houses were better than their previous ones.

APPENDIX C

Maps of Survey Neighborhoods

BOSTON

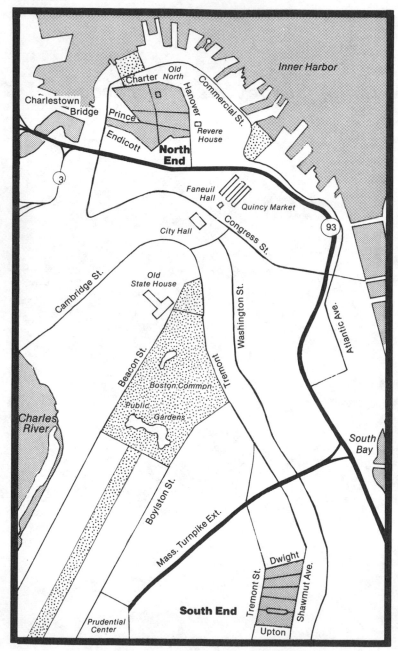

CINCINNATI

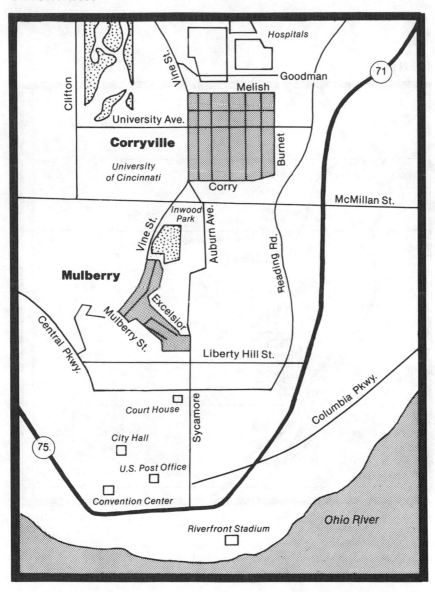

(DENVER)

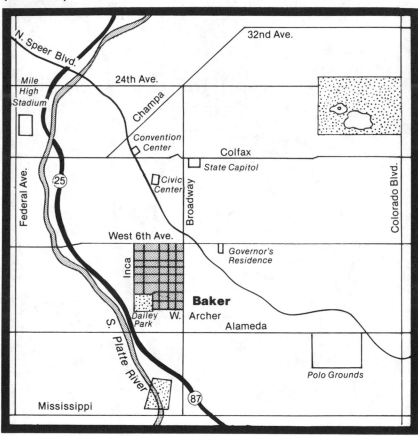

RICHMOND

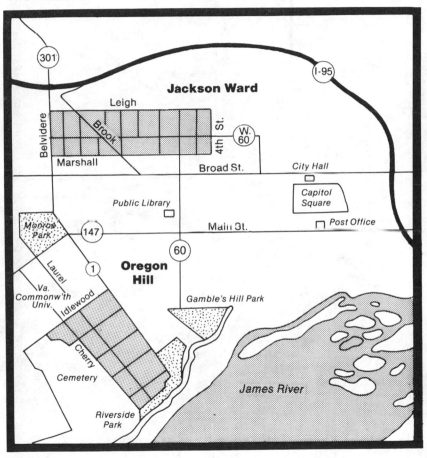

SEATTLE

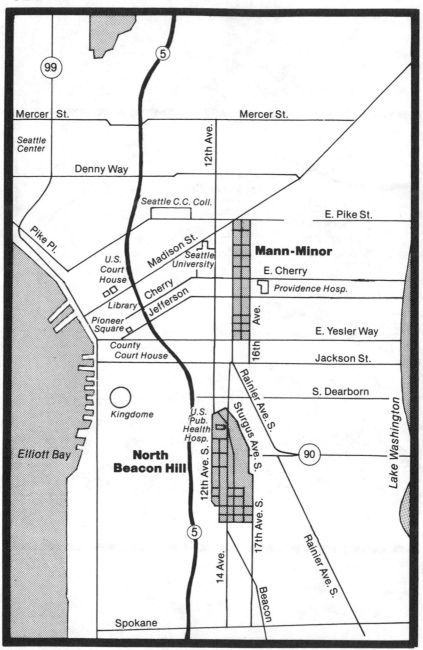

APPENDIX D

Survey Results by Summary Categories of Reasons for Moving

Table D-1 SOCIOECONOMIC CHARACTERISTICS OF MOVERS
(PERCENTAGES)

CHARACTERISTIC	REASON FOR MOVING					
	DISPLACE-MENT	JOB-RELATED	CHANGE IN HOUSING NEEDS	BETTER HOUSE	BETTER NEIGH-BORHOOD	OTHER
Over sixty-five years	13.9	12.8	4.0	11.9	18.0	19.5
Female-headed	33.3	29.7	28.5	45.0	42.6	28.0
Married	35.7	37.8	54.6	50.8	41.9	41.6
Nonwhite	46.1	28.6	43.7	60.0	44.3	31.6
Black	21.7	8.6	15.9	43.3	16.4	15.8
Hispanic	13.9	0	3.3	10.0	6.6	3.9
Asian	7.8	20.0	23.8	5.0	21.3	9.2
Unemployed	17.9	2.6	4.7	5.2	4.8	3.9
Completed 12th grade	63.4	84.5	76.1	70.0	69.5	75.1
Earning under $10,000	50.0	22.2	24.5	41.0	36.0	29.2
Earning over $25,000	5.9	22.2	21.6	15.4	10.0	17.2
Single-person households	33.6	35.9	21.9	21.7	30.6	24.7
Had lived in neighborhood over 5 years	36.2	18.0	29.1	51.8	37.1	39.0

Table D-2 SATISFACTION WITH NEW HOMES AND NEIGHBORHOODS

RATING	REASON FOR MOVING (PERCENTAGES)					
	DISPLACE-MENT	JOB-RELATED	CHANGE IN HOUSING NEEDS	BETTER HOUSE	BETTER NEIGH-BORHOOD	OTHER
New House Rating						
Excellent	15.7	23.7	26.1	21.9	32.3	32.4
Good	45.2	44.7	49.7	46.9	46.8	27.9
Fair	30.4	26.3	21.6	23.4	17.7	32.4
Poor	8.7	5.3	2.6	7.8	3.2	7.4
New Neighborhood Rating						
Excellent	19.1	15.8	24.2	20.3	35.5	30.4
Good	40.9	60.5	41.8	50.0	43.5	37.7
Fair	31.3	18.4	25.5	26.6	21.0	26.1
Poor	8.7	5.3	8.5	3.1	0.0	5.8
Comparison of Current Home with Previous One						
Much better	48.2	44.7	74.5	50.0	65.6	51.4
Slightly better	19.3	31.6	13.4	31.7	24.6	21.6
Same	16.7	13.2	6.0	13.3	6.6	13.5
Slightly worse	10.5	5.3	6.0	5.0	1.6	8.1
Much worse	5.3	5.3	0	0	1.6	5.4
Comparison of Current Neighborhood with Previous One						
Much better	33.3	45.7	39.7	27.3	71.4	49.2
Slightly better	23.0	22.9	20.6	29.5	19.6	16.4
Same	24.1	17.1	22.2	34.1	7.1	19.7
Slightly worse	14.9	5.7	13.5	4.5	1.8	11.5
Much worse	4.6	8.6	4.0	4.5	0	3.3

Table D-3 CHANGES IN HOUSING CHARACTERISTICS
(PERCENTAGES)

CHARACTERISTIC	REASON FOR MOVING					
	DISPLACE-MENT	JOB-RELATED	CHANGE IN HOUSING NEEDS	BETTER HOUSE	BETTER NEIGH-BORHOOD	OTHER
Median rent before move	$223	$214	$218	$166	$195	$178
Median rent after move	$188	$489	$277	$226	$235	$228
Percent increase in median rent	19%	129%	27%	36%	21%	21%
Median rent per room before move	$ 56	$ 62	$ 62	$ 41	$ 54	$ 54
Median rent per room after move	$ 56	$ 96	$ 66	$ 52	$ 72	$ 71
Percent increase in median rent per room	0	55%	6%	27%	33%	31%
Median persons per room before move	.51	.50	.60	.74	.60	.57
Median persons per room after move	.51	.49	.50	.62	.50	.50
Percent increase in median persons per room	0	-2%	-17%	-16%	-17%	-12%

Notes

1. The Setting for Urban Neighborhood Reinvestment

1. For a detailed discussion of these tests, see pages 68–69 and appendix B.

2. James W. Fossett and Richard P. Nathan, "The Prospects for Urban Revival," in *Urban Government Finance: Emerging Trends*, Roy Bahl, ed. (Beverly Hills, Calif.: Sage Publications, 1981).

2. Neighborhood Revitalization

1. Richard Ernie Reed, *Return to the City* (Garden City, N.Y.: Doubleday & Co., 1979), p. 14.

2. T. D. Allman, "The Urban Crisis Leaves Town," *Harper's*, December 1978, pp. 41–56.

3. Fossett and Nathan, "Prospects for Urban Revival," p. 22.

4. John L. Goodman, Jr., *Urban Residential Mobility: Places, People and Policy* (Washington, D.C.: Urban Institute, 1978), p. 3.

5. U.S. Department of Housing and Urban Development, "Whither or Whether Urban Distress—A Response" (Washington, D.C.: Department of Housing and Urban Development, 1979).

6. Dennis E. Gale, "The Back-to-the-City Movement . . . or Is It? A Survey of Recent Homebuyers in the Mount Pleasant Neighborhood of Washington, D.C." (Washington, D.C.: George Washington University, Department of Urban and Regional Planning, 1976), p. 10, and "The Back-to-the-City Movement Revisited: A Survey of Recent Homebuyers in the Capitol Hill Neighborhood of Washington, D.C." (Washington, D.C.: George Washington University, Department of Urban and Regional Planning, 1977), p. 14.

7. J. Thomas Black, "Private Market Housing Renovation in Central Cities: A U.L.I. Survey," *Urban Land*, November 1975, p. 7.

8. Franklin James, *Back to the City: An Appraisal of Housing Reinvestment and Population Change in Urban America* (Washington, D.C.: Urban Institute, 1977).

9. Ibid., p. 39.

10. Daphne Spain, "Indicators of Urban Revitalization: Racial and Socioeconomic Changes in Central-City Housing," in Shirley Bradway Laska and Daphne Spain, eds., *Back to the City: Issues in Neighborhood Renovation* (New York: Pergamon Press, 1980), p. 38.

11. Conrad Weiler and National Association of Neighborhoods, "Achieving Social and Economic Diversity in Inner-City Neighborhoods Through Increased Demand for City Housing by Middle-Income Persons" (Washington, D.C.: National Association of Neighborhoods, October 1978), p. 33.

12. Larry Long and Donald C. Dahmann, "Is Gentrification Narrowing the City-Suburb Income Gap?" (U.S. Bureau of the Census, Washington, D.C., September 1979, mimeo), pp. 10–11.

13. Susanna McBee, "Is There a National Back-to-the-City Trend? Probably Not," *Washington Post*, September 4, 1978, p. A-2.

14. See Alex Anas and Leon Moses, "Transportation and Land Use in the Mature Metropolis," in Charles L. Levin, ed., *The Mature Metropolis* (Lexington, Mass.: Lexington Books, 1978); and Peter Salins, "The Limits of Gentrification," *New York Affairs*, vol. 5, no. 4 (1979).

15. James, *Back to the City*, p. 229.

16. Martin D. Abravanel and Paul K. Mancini, "Attitudinal and Demographic Constraints," in Donald B. Rosenthal, ed., *Urban Revitalization* (Beverly Hills, Calif.: Sage Publications, 1980), p. 37.

17. R. Muth, *Cities and Housing* (Chicago: University of Chicago Press, 1969); William Alonso, *Location and Land Use* (Cambridge: M.I.T. Press, 1964); Edwin S. Mills, *Urban Economics* (Glenview, Ill.: Scott, Foresman, 1972).

18. Clifford R. Kern, "Upper Income Renaissance in the City: Its Sources and Implications for the City's Future" (Binghamton: Department of Economics, State University of New York at Binghamton, 1979).

19. Wendell Bell, "The City, the Suburb, and a Theory of Social Choice," in Scott Greer, ed., *The New Urbanization* (New York: St. Martin's Press, 1968), pp. 147–148.

20. U.S. Bureau of the Census, *Households and Families, by Type: March 1980 (Advance Report)*, Current Population Reports, Population Characteristics, Series P-20, No. 357 (Washington, D.C.: U.S. Government Printing Office, October 1980), p. 1.

21. William Alonso, "The Population Factor and Urban Structure," in U.S. Congress, House, Subcommittee on the City, Committee on Banking, Finance, and Urban Affairs, *How Cities Can Grow Old Gracefully* (Washington, D.C.: U.S. Government Printing Office, 1977), p. 36.

22. It has increased from 35 per 1,000 married persons in 1960 to 100 per 1,000 in 1980, an increase of almost 190 percent. The bulk of this increase has occurred in the past decade. U.S. Bureau of the Census, *Population Profile of the United States: 1980,* Current Population Reports, Population Characteristics, Series P-20, No. 363 (Washington, D.C.: U.S. Government Printing Office, June 1981), table 12.

23. U.S. Bureau of the Census, *Households and Families by Type*, table 3.

24. In 1960, the median age for men at marriage was 22.8 years; by 1979, the median had increased to 24.4 years. Similarly, the median age for women at marriage rose from 20.3 to 22.1 years. U.S. Bureau of the Census, *Marital*

Status and Living Arrangements: March 1979, Current Population Reports, Population Characteristics, Series P-20, No. 349 (Washington, D.C.: U.S. Government Printing Office, February 1980), table A.

25. Sternlieb and Hughes report that the average living unit in a city has fewer rooms than a unit in the suburbs. In 1976 the median number of rooms per unit in cities was 3.8 while for suburbs the number was 4.1. George Sternlieb and James Hughes, *America's Housing: Prospects and Problems* (New Brunswick, N.J.: Center for Urban Policy Research, Rutgers University, 1980), p. 123.

26. The number of births per 1,000 females has fallen from 120 in 1959 to 76 in 1979. Figure for 1959 computed from data in U.S. Bureau of the Census, *Marriage, Fertility, and Childspacing: August 1959*, Current Population Reports, Population Characteristics, Series P-20, No. 108 (Washington, D.C.: U.S. Government Printing Office, July 1961), tables 25 and 26. Figure for 1979, idem, *Fertility of American Women: June 1979*, Current Population Reports, Population Characteristics, Series P-20, No. 358 (Washington, D.C.: U.S. Government Printing Office, December 1980), table D.

27. U.S. Bureau of the Census, *Households and Families by Type*, table 2.

28. U.S. Bureau of the Census, *Population Profile of the United States: 1980*, Current Population Reports, Population Characteristics, Series P-20, No. 363 (Washington, D.C.: U.S. Government Printing Office, June 1981), table 21.

29. U.S. Department of Housing and Urban Development, *1979 Statistical Yearbook* (Washington, D.C.: U.S. Government Printing Office, November 1980), p. 263.

30. The Robert A. McNeil Corporation, "The American Housing Market: A National View," in U.S. Congress, Senate, Committee on Banking, Housing, and Urban Affairs, *Rental Housing, Hearing before the Subcommittee on Housing and Urban Affairs* (Washington, D.C.: U.S. Government Printing Office), 96th Congress, 2nd session, March 20, 1980, p. 90.

31. Rolf Goetze, "The Housing Bubble," *Working Papers for a New Society*, January-February 1981, p. 44.

32. Over the past ten years more than 366,000 rental units have been converted to condominiums, more than two-thirds of these conversions taking place from 1976 to 1979. U.S. Department of Housing and Urban Development, *The Conversion of Rental Housing to Condominiums and Cooperatives: A National Study of Scope, Causes and Impacts* (Washington, D.C.: U.S. Government Printing Office, June 1980), p. IV-6.

33. James, *Back to the City*, p. 67.

34. See, for example, George and Eunice S. Grier, *Displacement: Where Things Stand* (Bethesda, Md.: Grier Partnership, February 1981), or Sternlieb and Hughes, *America's Housing.*

35. Bernard J. Frieden, "The New Housing-Cost Problem," *The Public Interest*, no. 49 (fall 1977), p. 78.

36. The services sector includes transportation, communications, finance, insurance, real estate, business services, health, and education. See J. Thomas Black, "The Changing Economic Role of Central Cities and Suburbs," in Arthur P. Solomon, ed., *The Prospective City* (Cambridge: M.I.T. Press, 1980), pp. 102-110 for a brief discussion of this sector.

37. Ibid., p. 108.
38. Ibid., p. 109.
39. S. Gregory Lipton, "Evidence of Central City Revival," *American Institute of Planners Journal*, vol. 43, no. 2 (April 1977), p. 146.
40. For example, see Allman, "The Urban Crisis Leaves Town," and James David Besser, "Gentrifying the Ghetto," *The Progressive*, January 1979, p. 30.
41. B. Bruce-Briggs, "Gasoline Prices and the Suburban Way of Life," *Public Interest*, no. 37 (fall 1974), p. 136.
42. Kenneth Small, "Energy Scarcity and Urban Development Patterns," *International Regional Science Review*, vol. 5, no. 2 (1980), p. 115.
43. For example, see "HUD's Role in the Displacement of Inner City Low Income Residents," *Law Project Bulletin*, October/November 1978, p. 3; and Paul R. Dommel et al., *Decentralizing Community Development* (Washington, D.C.: U.S. Department of Housing and Urban Development, 1978), pp. 249-252.
44. Phillip L. Clay, *Neighborhood Renewal* (Lexington, Mass.: Lexington Books, 1979), p. 103.
45. Conrad Weiler, "Statement before the U.S. Senate Committee on Banking, Housing, and Urban Affairs," June 1977 (mimeo).
46. Robin E. Datel and Dennis J. Dingemans, "Historic Preservation and Urban Change," *Urban Geography*, vol. 1, no. 3 (July-September 1980), pp. 229-253.
47. Richard W. Travis, *Regional Components of the Recognition of Historic Places: Paper Number 3, Occasional Publications* (Urbana, Ill.: University of Illinois), p. 3, as cited in Datel and Dingemans, "Historic Preservation and Urban Change."
48. Advisory Council on Historic Preservation, *Report to the President and the Congress of the United States* (Washington, D.C.: U.S. Government Printing Office, 1980), p. 9.
49. Urban Policy Group, Advisory Council on Historic Preservation, *Remember the Neighborhoods: Conserving Neighborhoods through Historic Preservation Techniques* (Washington, D.C.: U.S. Government Printing Office, 1981), p. 3.
50. Advisory Council, *Report to the President*, p. 18.
51. Heritage Conservation and Recreation Service, *Federal Tax Provisions to Encourage Rehabilitation of Historic Buildings: An Assessment of Their Effect* (Washington, D.C.: U.S. Government Printing Office, August 1979), p. 2.
52. Ibid., p. 6.
53. According to statistics compiled by the FBI, from 1972 to 1979 crime in suburban areas increased by 46.7 percent while crimes in cities with populations in excess of 250,000 increased at a rate of only 30 percent over the eight-year span.
54. Quoted in William Severine Kowinski, "Suburbia: End of the Golden Age," *New York Times Magazine*, March 16, 1980, p. 16.
55. U.S. Department of Housing and Urban Development, *The 1978 HUD Survey of the Quality of Community Life: A Data Book 1978* (Washington, D.C.: U.S. Government Printing Office, 1978).

56. For example, see Reed, *Return to the City*, p. xi, and Nadine Brozan, "For Some Suburban Families, City Living Has Become Alluring," *New York Times*, February 20, 1979, p. C-5.

57. Frank F. DeGiovanni et al., "Private Market Revitalization: Its Characteristics and Consequences." Report prepared for Office of Policy Development and Research, Department of Housing and Urban Development (Research Triangle Park, N.C.: Research Triangle Institute, 1981).

58. Allen C. Goodman and Richard Weissbrod, *Housing Market Activity in South Baltimore: Immigration, Speculation, and Displacement* (Baltimore: The Johns Hopkins University, Center for Metropolitan Planning and Research, 1979).

59. Gale, "Back-to-the-City Movement," and also, Gale, "Back-to-the-City Movement Revisited."

60. Shirley B. Laska and Daphne Spain, "Anticipating Renovators' Demands: New Orleans," in Laska and Spain, eds., *Back to the City*.

61. DeGiovanni et al., "Private Market Revitalization."

62. Sonya M. Sands, "Population Change Due to Housing Renovation in the St. Paul's Ramsey Hill Area" (Master's thesis, University of Minnesota, Graduate School, 1979).

63. U.S. Bureau of the Census, and Office of Policy Development and Research, *Annual Housing Survey: 1978, Part D: Housing Characteristics of Recent Movers*, Current Housing Reports, Series H-150-78 (Washington, D.C.: U.S. Government Printing Office, May 1981).

64. Gale, "Back-to-the-City Movement," p. 10, and Gale, "Back-to-the-City Movement Revisited," p. 14.

65. James, *Back to the City*, p. 72.

66. Seattle Office of Policy Planning, Physical Planning Division, *Seattle Displacement Study* (Seattle: Seattle Office of Policy Planning, October 1979).

67. DeGiovanni et al., "Private Market Revitalization."

68. Herman C. Sieverding, "Displacement in Reinvestment Neighborhoods" (Undergraduate thesis, University of Cincinnati, Department of Planning, 1979).

69. Sands, "Population Change Due to Housing Renovation."

70. Laska and Spain, "Anticipating Renovators' Demands."

71. Christopher Winters, "The Geography of Rejuvenation in an Inner-City Neighborhood: The Upper West Side of Manhattan 1950-1977." Paper presented at the 73d Annual Meeting of the Association of American Geographers, 1977.

72. See Roman A. Cybriwsky, "Social Aspects of Neighborhood Change," *Annals of the Association of American Geographers*, vol. 68, no. 1 (March 1978); and Paul R. Levy, *Queen Village: The Eclipse of a Community* (Philadelphia: Institute for the Study of Civic Values, 1978); and DeGiovanni et al., "Private Market Revitalization."

73. Gale, "Back-to-the-City Movement" and "Back-to-the-City Movement Revisited."

74. Clay, *Neighborhood Renewal*, and Gale, "Back-to-the-City Movement Revisited."

75. Clay, *Neighborhood Renewal*, p. 18.

76. Ibid.

77. Clay, *Neighborhood Renewal*; Dennis E. Gale, "Middle-Class Resettlement in Older Urban Neighborhoods," *American Planning Association Journal*, July 1979, p. 301; Rolf Goetze, *Understanding Neighborhood Change: The Role of Expectations in Urban Revitalization* (Cambridge, Mass.: Ballinger Publishing Company, 1979); The National Urban Coalition, *Displacement: City Neighborhoods in Transition* (Washington, D.C.: The National Urban Coalition, 1978), p. 3; and Timothy Pattison, "The Process of Neighborhood Upgrading and Gentrification" (Master's thesis, Massachusetts Institute of Technology, Department of City Planning, June 1977).

78. DeGiovanni et al., "Private Market Revitalization," p. 273.

79. Weiler and National Association of Neighborhoods, "Achieving Social and Economic Diversity," pp. 83–85.

80. Phyllis Myers and Gordon Binder, *Neighborhood Conservation Lessons from Three Cities* (Washington, D.C.: The Conservation Foundation, 1977), p. 15.

81. Annmarie Sasdi, "From Slum to Gold Coast: Residential Revitalization for Upper-Income Families" (Undergraduate thesis, Princeton University, School of Architecture and Urban Planning, 1978), p. 11.

82. Ibid., p. 41.

83. Myers and Binder, *Neighborhood Conservation Lessons*, p. 19.

84. DeGiovanni et al., "Private Market Revitalization," p. xxi.

85. Ibid., p. 284.

86. Sasdi, "From Slum to Gold Coast," p. 6.

87. Weiler and National Association of Neighborhoods, "Achieving Social and Economic Diversity," pp. 15–16.

88. Ibid., p. 11.

89. Advisory Council on Historic Preservation, *The Contribution of Historic Preservation to Urban Revitalization* (Washington, D.C.: U.S. Government Printing Office, January 1979), p. 9.

90. Clay, *Neighborhood Renewal*, p. 22.

91. Myers and Binder, *Neighborhood Conservation Lessons*, p. 21.

92. The neighborhoods may be experiencing high turnover because of the influx of upper-income households who moved in shortly before the 1980 census was taken. Census figures for that year will provide a more accurate indication of whether turnover has increased or decreased following revitalization.

93. Gale, "Back-to-the-City Movement," p. 8, and "Back-to-the-City Movement Revisited," p. 12.

94. DeGiovanni et al., "Private Market Revitalization," p. xxviii.

95. Ibid., p. 174.

96. Advisory Council on Historic Preservation, *Contribution of Historic Preservation*, p. 11.

97. City of Cincinnati, Division of Police, *1960 Annual Report of the Division of Police* (Cincinnati Police Division, June 1961), table 86, and *1979 Annual Report of the Division of Police* (Cincinnati Police Division, June 1980), table 86.

98. Gale, "Back-to-the-City Movement," p. 8, and "Back-to-the-City Movement Revisited," p. 9.

99. Richard Netzer, "Impact of the Property Tax: Its Economic Implications for Urban Problems." Research report by National Commission on

Urban Problems to the Joint Economic Committee, 90th Congress, 2nd session (Washington, D.C.: U.S. Government Printing Office, 1968), p. 21.

100. George E. Peterson, "The Property Tax and Low-Income Housing Markets," in George E. Peterson, ed., *Property Tax Reform* (Washington, D.C.: Urban Institute, 1973), p. 113.

101. Ibid., pp. 110–112.

102. In each of the three neighborhoods, property tax assessments over a twenty-year period (1960 to 1980) were compared to citywide assessment totals for the same period. For each neighborhood, assessments were recorded from a sample of properties, chosen by selecting every *nth* block in the neighborhood and including all properties on those streets. Tax abatements and exemptions were deducted from the tax assessment of each property included in the sample. Citywide totals (less exemptions and abatements) were from local assessors.

103. "Redeveloping Neighborhoods Will Be among the Hardest Hit," *Baltimore Evening Sun*, December 14, 1978.

104. For example, see Myers and Binder, *Neighborhood Conservation Lessons*; and "Property Tax Rise Opposed in Detroit," *The New York Times*, March 23, 1980.

105. DeGiovanni et al., "Private Market Revitalization," p. 293.

106. Ibid., p. 298.

107. James, *Back to the City*, p. 256.

108. Carol Richards and Jonathan Rowe, "Restoring a City: Who Pays the Price," *Working Papers for a New Society*, vol. 4, no. 4 (1977), p. 54.

109. Ibid.

110. Clay, *Neighborhood Renewal*, p. 60.

111. Homer Hoyt Institute, "An Evaluation of the Study Called 'Facts About Real Estate Speculation'" (Washington, D.C.: Homer Hoyt Institute, 1975), p. 5.

112. Richards and Rowe, "Restoring a City," p. 54.

113. Council of the District of Columbia, Committee on Finance and Revenue, "Facts About Real Estate Speculation," 1975, p. 5.

114. Levy, *Queen Village*, p. 61.

115. Cybriwsky, "Social Aspects of Neighborhood Change," p. 32.

116. Ibid.

117. Barry Merchant, "Dislocation of Disadvantaged Residents" (Princeton, N.J.: Princeton University, Woodrow Wilson School, 1978).

118. Jon Pynoos, Robert Schafer, and Chester Hartman, eds., *Housing Urban America* (New York: Aldine Publishing Company, 1980).

119. Bernard J. Frieden and Arthur P. Solomon, *The Nation's Housing: 1975 to 1985* (Cambridge: Joint Center for Urban Studies, 1977), p. 95.

120. This shrinking of housing options is nowhere more visible than in the long-time staple housing source for low-income single persons—the single-room-occupancy (SRO) hotel. Across the country the number of units in SROs is declining. In some areas they are being converted to luxury condominiums, while in others they are abandoned by owners unable to afford taxes and maintenance costs. In New York City, SROs have disappeared at an alarming rate. Because of this—and other forces at work—it is estimated that as many as 36,000 of the city's most vulnerable residents, the low-income elderly, now sleep in the streets. Ellen Baxter and Kim Hopper,

Private Lives/Public Spaces: Homeless Adults on the Streets of New York (New York: Community Services Society, Institute for Social Welfare Research, 1981), pp. 8-9.

3. Displacement

1. George and Eunice Grier, *Displacement*, pp. 10-11.
2. Ibid., p. 13.
3. Ibid., p. 15.
4. Fergus Bordewich, "The Future of New York: A Tale of Two Cities," *New York*, July 23, 1979, pp. 32-40.
5. Interview by author with Wayne Hazel, Federal Home Loan Bank Board, August 1981.
6. M. Carl Holman, testimony before the U.S. Senate, Committee on Banking, Housing and Urban Affairs, July 7-8, 1977, *Neighborhood Diversity* (Washington, D.C.: U.S. Government Printing Office, 1977), p. 190.
7. Eileen Zeitz, *Private Urban Renewal* (Lexington, Mass.: Lexington Books, 1979), pp. 114-116.
8. Sasdi, "From Slum to Gold Coast," p. 74.
9. For example, see Parkman Center for Urban Affairs, *Young Professionals and City Neighborhoods* (Boston: Parkman Center for Urban Affairs, 1977), p. 4; Bordewich, "The Future of New York," p. 38; and Weiler and National Association of Neighborhoods, "Achieving Social and Economic Diversity," p. 25.
10. Dempsey J. Travis, "How Whites Are Taking Back Black Neighborhoods," *Ebony*, September 1978, p. 73.
11. For example, see Trace Gibson, "Claim Housing Mobility Program Designed to Move Inner-City Blacks to Suburbs," *Philadelphia Tribune*, August 28, 1979.
12. Trace Gibson, "Housing Mobility Program Is the Center of Controversy," *Philadelphia Tribune*, September 21, 1979.
13. Mark Fried, "Grieving for a Lost Home: Psychological Costs of Relocation," in James Q. Wilson, ed., *Urban Renewal: The Record and the Controversy* (Cambridge: M.I.T. Press, 1966), p. 362.
14. U.S. Congress, Senate, Committee on Banking, Housing and Urban Affairs, Subcommittee on Housing and Urban Affairs, *Condominium Housing Issues* (Washington, D.C.: U.S. Government Printing Office, June 1979), p. 314.
15. For example, see Betty Collier et al., "From Theory to Praxis: An Analysis of Some Aspects of the Displacement Process in the District of Columbia" (Washington: University of the District of Columbia, Department of Economics, 1979); Bordewich, "The Future of New York"; and Travis, "Whites Taking Back Black Neighborhoods," pp. 72-82.
16. Seattle Office of Policy Planning, Physical Planning Division, *Seattle Displacement Study* (Seattle: Office of Policy Planning, October 1979).
17. Sandra J. Newman and Michael S. Owen, "Residential Displacement in the U.S., 1970-1977." Paper prepared for the U.S. Department of Housing and Urban Development, Office of Policy Development and Research, 1980.

18. Michael H. Schill, "Displacement: A Systematic Study of Those Displaced by Private Action" (Princeton University, Woodrow Wilson School, 1978).

19. National Institute for Advanced Studies, "Market Generated Displacement: A Single City Case Study." Draft report prepared for the U.S. Department of Housing and Urban Development (Washington, D.C.: National Institute for Advanced Studies, 1980).

20. Gloria Cousar, U.S. Department of Housing and Urban Development, "Bulletin on HUD Estimates of Displacement and Pertinent Program Information." Presentation prepared for National Urban League Conference, Los Angeles, August 1978.

21. Richard LeGates and Chester Hartman, "Gentrification-Related Displacement," *Clearinghouse Review*, vol. 15, no. 3 (July 1981), p. 220.

22. Newman and Owen, "Residential Displacement in the U.S.," pp. 48–49.

4. Methodology and Description of Study Areas

1. Michael H. Schill, *Neighborhood Reinvestment and Displacement: A Working Paper* (Princeton, N.J.: Princeton University, Princeton Urban and Regional Research Center, 1981).

2. Phillip L. Clay, "Neighborhood Reinvestment Without Displacement: A Handbook For Local Government" (Cambridge: M.I.T., Department of Urban Studies and Planning, 1979), p. 40.

3. Owner-occupants were not excluded from the Boston survey, since the resident listing did not provide information on household tenure.

4. Michael Schill's interview with William Cozzens, National Institute for Advanced Studies, June 1980.

5. For example, see Arnold Abrams, "Below the Bottom Rung," *Newsday*, October 15, 1981; Robin Herman, "New York Trying to Add Shelters For Its Homeless," *New York Times*, July 26, 1982; Randy Young, "The Homeless: The Shame of the City," *New York*, December 21, 1981; Baxter and Hopper, *Private Lives/Public Spaces*.

6. See Virginia Culver, "Church Open To Wanderers," *Denver Post*, February 13, 1982; Judith Cummings, "Increase in Homeless People Tests U.S. Cities' Will to Cope," *New York Times*, May 3, 1982; George Raine, "Energy States Turning Cold To Transients," *New York Times*, February 2, 1982; Carol Saline, "Dealing At Street Level," *Philadelphia*, February 1982.

7. Other major causes of homelessness are the deinstitutionalization of the mentally ill and rising unemployment.

8. Eric G. Moore, *Residential Mobility in the City* (Washington, D.C.: Commission on College Geography, Association of American Geographers, 1972).

9. U.S. Department of Housing and Urban Development, *Residents' Satisfaction in HUD-Assisted Housing: Design and Management Factors* (Washington, D.C.: U.S. Government Printing Office, March 1979), pp. 1–5.

10. Angus Campbell, *The Sense of Well-Being in America: Recent Patterns and Trends* (New York: McGraw-Hill Book Company, 1981), pp. 157–158.

11. U.S. Department of Commerce, Bureau of the Census, 1980 Apportionment Population File (computer tape). R. L. Polk & Company, Canvass Tapes for Cincinnati, Denver, Richmond, and Seattle, 1970–1980.

12. Bonnie Heudorfer, *Condominium Development in Boston* (Boston: Boston Redevelopment Authority, September 1980), p. 13.

13. While the city's population has decreased 19 percent since 1960, its population in the twenty- to thirty-four-year-old cohort increased 24 percent during the same period. U.S. Bureau of the Census, *Census of Population: 1970, Characteristics of the Population, Number of Inhabitants*, vol. 1, part A (Washington, D.C.: U.S. Government Printing Office, 1972), pp. 15–16.

14. OKM Associates, "Revitalization Without Displacement: A Discussion of and Challenge to the New Boston" (Boston: OKM Associates, January 1981), p. 8.

15. Heudorfer, *Condominium Development in Boston*, p. 16.

16. Ibid., p. 3.

17. Mitchell C. Lynch, "Boston's Renaissance Brightens Downtown But Masks Many Ills," *Wall Street Journal*, November 13, 1980, p. 1.

18. Boston 200 Commission, *The North End* (Boston: Boston 200 Commission, 1976), and Kathleen Kilgore, "A Tale of Two Neighborhoods," *The New Englander*, March 1979, p. 19.

19. Boston Redevelopment Authority, *District Planning Program* (Boston: Boston Redevelopment Authority, June 1975).

20. Curtis Hartman, "The North End Forever," *Boston*, 1978, p. 78.

21. Ibid.

22. Ibid.

23. Boston Redevelopment Authority, *North End Waterfront: District Profile and Proposed 1978–1980 Neighborhood Improvement Program* (Boston: Boston Redevelopment Authority, 1977), p. 10.

24. Boston Redevelopment Authority, *District Planning Program*, p. 10.

25. Ibid., p. 17.

26. Karen Buglass, "Condominium Update: January through August 1980," Boston Redevelopment Authority Research Department, March 1981.

27. Hartman, "The North End Forever," p. 55.

28. Diane Dumanoski, "Boston's Italian North End; Changing Immigrant Neighborhood Still is 'Home' to Farm Resident," *American Preservation*, February/March 1979, p. 44.

29. Elizabeth M. Seifel, "Displacement: The Negative Environmental Impact of Urban Renewal in the South End of Boston" (Master's thesis, M.I.T., June 1979), p. 12.

30. Ibid., p. 13.

31. Ibid., p. 2.

32. Ibid., p. 17.

33. Ibid., p. 122.

34. Ibid., p. 54.

35. Ibid., p. 130.

36. Ibid., p. 65.

37. Buglass, "Condominium Update."

38. Interview with William Apgar, Jr., July 1981.

39. Ibid.

40. Deborah A. Auger, "The Politics of Revitalization in Gentrifying Neighborhoods," *American Planning Association Journal*, October 1979, pp. 515–522.

41. "Viewpoint SEPAC," *South End News*, December 20, 1980, p. 4.

42. "Background Information on Cincinnati" (memo, no author given).

43. Debbie Chapin, address to "Leadership Cincinnati" program, sponsored by Cincinnati Chamber of Commerce, February 1979.

44. Ibid.

45. Ibid.

46. Steven Rosen, "You Can Get a Building for Nothing," *Cincinnati Enquirer*, May 14, 1981.

47. Michael Miller et al., "Displacement Memo" (Cincinnati, 1979), p. 2.

48. Dave Krieger, "Council Okays New Measure to Assist Displaced Tenants," *Cincinnati Enquirer*, July 3, 1980.

49. Jim Sluzewski, "Community Undergoing Quiet Change," *Cincinnati Enquirer*, December 18, 1978.

50. Real Estate Research Corporation, "Comprehensive Housing Strategy Final Report," Cincinnati, July 1974.

51. City of Cincinnati, "Neighborhood Profile Memo, Corryville," 1979.

52. Sluzewski, "Community Undergoing Quiet Change."

53. Interview by author with real estate agent, Kathy Laker, August 1981.

54. Unpublished data from City of Cincinnati, Office of Planning.

55. Mortgage disclosure information supplied by Cincinnati Savings Association, Home Federal Savings and Loan Association, Eagle Savings Association, and Home State Savings Association.

56. Laker interview.

57. Sluzewski, "Community Undergoing Quiet Change."

58. City of Cincinnati, "Over-the-Rhine Existing Condition Report," September 1973.

59. John Eckberg, "Over-the-Rhine Task Force Blasted as Waste Of Time," *Cincinnati Enquirer*, March 19, 1981.

60. Jane Ransom, "Dismal Statistics Fail Over-the-Rhine Businesses," *Cincinnati Enquirer*, October 11, 1980.

61. Rosen, "You Can Get a Building for Nothing."

62. Ransom, "Dismal Statistics."

63. City of Cincinnati, "Neighborhood Profile: Over-the-Rhine," memo, 1979.

64. Mortgage disclosure information supplied by Cincinnati Savings Association, Home Federal Savings and Loan Association, Eagle Savings Association, and Home State Savings Association.

65. Laker interview.

66. James M. Rubenstein, "Displacement in a Cincinnati Neighborhood" (Oxford, Ohio: Miami University, November 1980).

67. Dave Krieger, "Hoskins' Pleas Help Sway Vote on Historic District," *Cincinnati Enquirer*, October 17, 1980.

68. U.S. Bureau of the Census, *Census of Population: 1970 Characteristics of the Population, Number of Inhabitants*, vol. 1, part A (Washington, D.C.: U.S. Government Printing Office, 1972), table 13.

69. George Bardwell, "Metro Denver Population Statistics: 1970–1980," in "Community Housing . . . Community Schools," report of a community conference, January 17, 1981, sponsored by the Community Resource Center, at the University of Colorado at Denver.

70. Interview with Bernie Jones, July 1981.

71. Bardwell, "Metro Denver Population Statistics," p. 22.

72. Denver Housing Authority spokesperson, July 1981.

73. Marty Flahive and Steve Gordon, "Residential Displacement in Denver: A Research Report" (Denver: City of Denver, Joint Administration Council Committee of Housing, May 1979), p. 1.

74. "West Side Neighborhood Plan: Part of the Comprehensive Plan for Denver." Draft, July 1980, pp. 6–7.

75. Ibid., p. 13.

76. Ibid., p. 13.

77. Ibid., p. 13.

78. Jones interview.

79. Flahive and Gordon, *Residential Displacement in Denver*, map II.

80. U.S. Bureau of the Census, *Census of Population: 1970 Characteristics of the Population, Number of Inhabitants*, vol. 1, part A (Washington, D.C.: U.S. Government Printing Office, 1972).

81. Barton-Aschman Associates and Clare Newman Anderson and Associates, *Central Wards/Jackson Ward and Oregon Hill Neighborhood Planning Study, Technical Report* (Richmond: City Department of Planning and Community Development, undated), p. 19.

82. Interview with Gene Winter, Department of Economic Development, August 1981.

83. Winter interview.

84. Unless otherwise cited, data on Jackson Ward in this section are from Barton-Aschman Associates and Clare Newman Anderson and Associates, *Central Wards*.

85. Interview with Peter Roggemann, July 1981.

86. Nita Jones, "The Ongoing Attraction of Urban Homesteading," *Richmond Magazine*, September 1980.

87. Roggemann interview.

88. Interview with Jean Boyea, July 1981.

89. Jerry Turner, "Reverse White Flight," *Richmond Afro-American*, November 1, 1980, pp. 62–64.

90. Unless otherwise cited, data on Oregon Hill are from Barton-Aschman Associates and Clare Newman Anderson and Associates, *Central Wards*.

91. Roggemann interview.

92. Interview with Jody McWilliams, William Byrd Community House, July 1981.

93. Ibid.

94. U.S. Bureau of the Census, *Census of Population: 1970 Characteristics of the Population, Number of Inhabitants*, vol. 1, part A (Washington, D.C.: U.S. Government Printing Office, 1972).

95. Interview with Steven Sheppard, director of neighborhood planning, city of Seattle, July 1981.

96. Seattle Office of Policy Planning, *Seattle Displacement Study*, p. 7.

97. A. Phillip Andrus et al., *Seattle* (Cambridge, Mass.: Ballinger Publishing Co. 1976), p. 15.

98. David C. Hodge, "Inner-City Revitalization and Displacement: The New Urban Future." Washington Public Policy Notes (Seattle: University of Washington, Institute of Governmental Research, summer 1979), p. ii.

99. Ibid., p. 11.

100. Seattle Real Estate Research Committee, "Real Estate Research Report: Seattle-Everett SMSA: King and Snohomish Counties," vol. 31, no. 1 (spring 1980), p. 13.

101. Ibid., p. 11.

102. Hodge, "Inner-City Revitalization and Displacement," p. 79.

103. Interview with Jeff Spelman of Southeast Effective Development, July 1981.

104. Lee Moriwaki, "The Changing Face of the Central Area," *Seattle Times*, June 7, 1980, p. 1.

105. Seattle Office of Policy Planning, "Housing Condition Trends, City of Seattle: 1974 and 1978," Current Planning Research Report No. 40 (January 1979), p. 3.

106. Spelman interview.

107. R. L. Polk & Co., "Polk Profile of Change, Garfield Community, 1976–77, 1974–77" (Seattle: Seattle Office of Policy Planning, undated).

108. Madison-Jackson Economic Development Council, "Mad-Jac Reports," undated.

109. Seattle Office of Policy Planning, "Housing Condition Trends," p. 6.

110. U.S. census data in table 7.

111. Sheppard interview.

112. Spelman interview.

113. Lee Moriwaki, "Racial Migration Stood Out Clearly in Recent Census, More Whites Move to Central Area, Blacks Shift Toward Rainier Valley," *Seattle Times*, June 7, 1981, p. 3.

114. Interview with Gary Clark, Department of Community Development, Seattle, July 1981.

115. R. L. Polk & Co., "Polk Profile of Change: Beacon Community, 1976–77, 1974–77" (Seattle: Seattle Office of Policy Planning, undated), p. 8.

116. Office of Community Development, Office of Neighborhood Planning Report, "North Beacon Hill," January, 1977.

117. Ibid., p. 1.

118. Spelman interview.

119. Sheppard interview.

120. Spelman interview.

5. Results of the Displacement Study

1. See pages 58–59.

2. One explanation for the overrepresentation of Hispanic-headed households in the displaced sample is that a large proportion of the Hispanic movers lived in Denver's Baker neighborhood, the study area with the highest displacement rate.

3. The poverty level was computed as follows: households with one or two persons—less than $5,000 per year; households with three persons—less than $6,999 per year; households with four, five, and six persons—less than $10,000 per year; households with seven or more persons—less than $15,000 per year. This index is a modified version of the levels specified by the Census Bureau for 1980.

4. This is deduced from the fact that HISPAN, which represents Hispanic-headed households, has a coefficient of 0.66, which is the largest in the equation. One may use the coefficients as an indicator of the importance of the associated variables in predicting the dependent variable.

5. The possibility that the sample of outmovers might be biased toward overrepresentation of households that relocated within the city from which they moved would not substantially alter the conclusion that the displaced tend to stay closer to their original neighborhood than the nondisplaced. To the contrary, such a bias would understate the difference between the displaced and nondisplaced, because it could be expected that those households moving beyond city limits would do so voluntarily rather than due to displacement.

6. Newman and Owen, "Residential Displacement in the U.S., 1970–1977," p. 24.

7. For a discussion of this model see Jan Kmenta, *Elements of Econometrics* (New York: Macmillan Publishing Co., 1971), chapter 11, section 1.

8. For a description of this estimation procedure, see S. M. Goldfeld and R. E. Quandt, *Nonlinear Methods in Econometrics* (Amsterdam: North-Holland Publishing Co., 1972), chapter 2.

9. The properties of this test are discussed in Goldfeld and Quandt, *Nonlinear Methods in Econometrics*, chapter 2. The test statistic is the natural logarithm of the ratio of the likelihood function of the restricted equation, i.e., the equation with the relevant variables excluded, to the likelihood function of the unrestricted equation. This statistic is distributed as a chi-square with r degrees of freedom, where r is the number of variables which are dropped.

6. Neighborhood Reinvestment, Displacement, and Public Policy

1. U.S. Congress, House of Representatives, "Conference Report on Housing and Community Development Amendments of 1978," October 14, 1978, p. 46.

2. David Alpern et al., "A City Revival?" *Newsweek*, January 25, 1979, p. 30.

3. Robert Embry, testimony before the U.S. Senate Committee on Banking, Housing, and Urban Affairs, *Neighborhood Diversity*, p. 28.

4. U.S. Department of Housing and Urban Development, *Displacement Report: Final* (Washington, D.C.: U.S. Government Printing Office, December 1979), p. i.

5. The Bureau of National Affairs, Inc., "CDBG Field Notice Requires Affordable, Sanitary Housing for Displaced Families," *Housing and Development Reporter*, vol. 8, no. 36 (February 2, 1981), p. 733.

6. "CDBG Field Notice Cuts Low-Moderate Income Benefits Test; Loosens Many Requirements," ibid. (May 25, 1981), p. 1082.

7. William A. Witte, "Reinvestment: The Federal Status," *Journal of Housing*, October 1979, p. 460.

8. In another study, the Princeton Urban and Regional Research Center is evaluating the effects on state and local governments and the people they serve of the cutbacks in domestic programs and related changes in national policy made in fiscal year 1982. The first book on this study contains extensive information on the urban policies and programs affected. See John W. Ellwood, ed., *Reductions in U.S. Domestic Spending: How They Affect State and Local Governments* (New Brunswick, N.J.: Transaction Books, 1982), p. 341.

9. Department of Housing and Urban Development, *Displacement Report: Final*, p. 15.

10. Statement by Michael Kane, Official Transcript, "Conference on Displacement, September 28, 1978" (Washington, D.C.: Department of Housing and Urban Development, 1978), p. 184.

11. Housing Association of Delaware Valley, "North Philadelphia—The Vanishing Core," Philadelphia, March 1975; and Bay Area Planners Network, "RAP in the Tenderloin," San Francisco, June 1977.

12. Phillip L. Clay, "Inventory and Assessment of Local Activities to Deal with Displacement of Low- and Moderate-Income Families as a Result of Reinvestment in Inner-City Neighborhoods: A Report on Task I of a Project for the Office of the Assistant Secretary of the U.S. Department of Housing and Urban Development," Massachusetts Institute of Technology, August 19, 1978, p. 19.

13. Ibid.; and National Center for Urban Ethnic Affairs, "Displacement Handbook" (Washington, D.C.: National Center for Urban Ethnic Affairs, draft 1978).

14. For information on the New York State program, see U.S. Senate, *Neighborhood Diversity*. For information on the St. Louis program, see National Urban Coalition, *Neighborhood Transition Without Displacement* (Washington, D.C.: National Urban Coalition, 1980).

15. Clay, "Inventory and Assessment Report," pp. 8 and 12.

16. Joyce B. Seigel, "Tenant Cooperation Is Established to Fend off Displacement," *Journal of Housing*, August/September 1979, pp. 402-405.

17. George Sternlieb et al., *Fort Lee Rent Control* (New Brunswick, N. J.: Center for Urban Policy Research, 1975).

18. John Gilderbloom, *Moderate Rent Control: The Experiences of U.S. Cities* (Washington, D.C.: Conference on Alternative State and Local Policies, May 1980), p. 32. See also, idem, "Moderate Rent Control," *Urban Affairs Quarterly*, vol. 17, no. 2 (December 1981), pp. 123-142; and George Sternlieb, "Comment," ibid., pp. 143-145.

19. Ellwood, ed., *Reductions in U.S. Domestic Spending*.

Index

homes, 7, 53, 54, 58, 59, 65, 112–13, 115, 116, 118, 119, 122

Demography. *See* Population
Denver, 2, 123; Baker, 3, 61, 85–86, 106, 111, 158, 176n.2; Denver Center for Community Design, 85; Denver Regional Council of Governments, 86; survey of displacement in, 61, 63, 84–86
Department of Housing and Urban Development (HUD), 134, 135–36; funding of antidisplacement organizations by, 72; funding of housing by, 76; grant to NIAS from, 55, 56; 1978 survey of the quality of community life by, 13; 1979 working paper by, 10; regional mobility program of, 51
Destabilization, neighborhood, 49, 51–52
Detroit, 12
Developers, real estate, 20, 29, 41, 100, 120
Disinvestment, 13, 47, 81, 119, 142
Displacement, 12–13; approaches to study of, 53, 54, 55, 60; causes of, 42, 43, 45, 46, 47–49, 55, 59, 64, 67, 105, 106–11, 117–20, 122, 136, 137, 170n.120 (*see also* Households; Housing; Rent); characteristics of those affected by, 57–58, 59, 103–11, 117–20, 122–23, 136, 153, 176n.2 (*see also* Educational level; Employment; Ethnicity; Households; Income levels; Marital status; Race); consequences of, 1, 2, 7, 8, 46, 47, 49–53, 66–67, 105, 107, 112–13, 133, 137, 142, 170n.120 (*see also* Hardship; Location; Relocation; Rent); definition of, 46–47, 54, 64–65, 70, 122; effect on, of the economy, 49, 72, 133; and the elderly, 52–53, 57, 73–74, 103, 104, 107, 110, 117, 118, 119, 122, 170n.120; fear of, 139; magnitude of, 1, 7, 46, 57, 59, 120, 133, 142; methodological obstacles to study of, 1–2, 3, 4, 53, 54, 55, 56, 57, 64, 65–70, 153–54; minimization of, 29, 30, 134–38, 139, 140; opposition to, 72, 76, 78, 84, 86, 90, 93, 135, 136–39; pilot study of, 2, 60; as a political issue, 136–37, 138–39; psychological trauma from, 49, 52, 118, 120; survey of, 73, 74, 76, 77, 78, 83–84, 85, 86, 90, 93, 99, 102–31. *See also* Government, federal;

Government, local; Government, state; Hardship; Households, displaced; Outmovers; Probit analysis; Public policy; Survey
Divorce, 17, 165n.22
Downtown development, 5

Economic Development Administration (EDA), 86
Economic resegregation, 49, 50
Economy: effect of, on displacement, 49, 72, 133; effect of, on older cities, 10, 12, 21; effect of, on reinvestment, 21, 30, 31, 48, 55, 90, 138, 142; effect on, of reinvestment, 33, 36, 38, 43, 45, 139; of survey neighborhoods, 71, 72, 73, 74, 76, 81, 88, 89, 92, 95–96, 99, 100
Educational level: as a factor in displacement, 47, 58, 103, 117, 119; as a factor in hardship, 104; as a factor in participation in reinvestment, 15, 72; of outmovers, 108, 110, 121, 123; of residents in reinvestment neighborhoods, 29, 32, 33, 47
Elderly: displacement of, 52–53, 57, 73–74, 103, 104, 107, 110, 117, 118, 119, 122, 170n.120; tax assistance to, 137
Employment: displaced persons' status of, 7, 103, 111, 118, 122; homeless persons' status of, 172n.7; inmovers' level of, 29, 47, 51; level of, and hardship, 7, 116, 119; level of, in survey neighborhoods, 71–100 passim; location of opportunities for, 4, 10, 12, 15, 16, 19, 21–22, 36, 45, 166n.36; outmovers' level of, 3, 51; as a reason to relocate, 105, 106, 108, 110
Energy: Denver as a center of, 84, 85; effect of rising costs of, 5, 22–23
Ethnicity: of displaced households, 111, 118, 122, 123, 176n.2; idealized, for neighborhoods, 119; of outmovers, 108, 109, 122, 123; in survey neighborhoods, 3, 72, 74, 77, 80, 84, 85, 95, 99, 100

"Familism," 17, 19
Federal National Mortgage Association, 23
Fiscal distress, 10, 12
"Flipping," 42–43, 137

Gentrification, 1, 12, 136, 139. *See also* Reinvestment

Government, federal, 4–5, 24; community development funds of, 23, 81, 86, 89, 135, 137, 138; as employer, 88, 100; funding of reinvestment by, 3, 5, 23, 32, 33, 36; policies of, 44, 51, 178n.8; response of, to displacement, 134–36; role of, in community development, 86, 134; role of, in reinvestment, 7, 23, 46; role of, in site improvements, 77; tax policies of, 20, 23, 24, 25

Government, local, 178n.8; disbursement of rehabilitation funds by, 81, 140; as employer, 88; enforcement of codes by, 47; funding of reinvestment by, 3, 5, 36, 73, 100; response of, to displacement, 136–38; role of, in assisting displaced households, 120, 135, 138, 139, 140, 141; role of, in community development, 86, 89, 100, 138, 140; role of, in reinvestment, 7, 31, 46, 73, 138–39; role of, in resisting displacement, 76, 77, 84, 85, 135, 140; role of, in site improvements, 74, 100, 139; tax policies of, 24, 25

Government, state, 178n.8; as employer, 88; response of, to displacement, 137–38; role of, in resisting displacement, 135

Hardship, definition of, for survey, 65, 70, 104, 115; and displacement, 7, 47, 112–13, 114–15, 116–17, 119, 120, 135, 139, 153–54

Harvard-M.I.T. Joint Center for Urban Studies, 44

Heritage Conservation and Recreation Service, 25

Historic preservation, 30, 36, 38, 84, 89; attitudes toward, 45, 84; tax benefits of, 24, 25; trend toward, 24–25

Homelessness, 66–67, 170n.120, 172n.7

Homeowners: desire to become, as a reason for relocation, 104, 105; effect on long-term, of displacement, 47–48; effect on long-term, of reinvestment, 29–30, 33, 38, 41, 47; exclusion of, from survey, 62, 64; first-time, 27–28, 86; helping tenants become, 135, 137, 140, 141; increase in number of, 19, 37; number of, compared with number of tenants, 30, 37; replacement by, of tenants, 48, 75; tax deductions for, 20, 23

Homer Hoyt Institute, 42

Households, displaced: assistance for, 120, 133, 134, 135, 137–38 (*see also* Government, local); compared with voluntary outmovers, 103–10, 111, 113–15, 119, 177n.5top; view by, of new housing and neighborhood, 55, 58–59, 65, 70, 104, 112, 113–16, 117, 118, 119, 121–22, 133, 162

Households, female-headed, 18, 19, 78, 81, 89, 90, 93, 107–8, 111, 122

Households, higher-income: demands by, for reinvestment, 31; effect of, on reinvestment neighborhoods, 33, 38, 46, 47, 49, 138; increases in number of, in reinvestment neighborhoods, 32, 47, 138, 169n.92; influx of, to urban neighborhoods, 7, 9, 11, 13, 17, 23, 27, 30, 33, 44; loss of, by cities, 10, 120; prediction of location of, by bid rent curve, 14; reaction toward, of long-term residents, 29–30, 43; as tenants, 48; undersampling of, in survey, 69

Households, shape of: as a factor in displacement, 58, 65, 117; as a factor in housing needs, 105; as a factor in increases in number of households, 17, 18; as a factor in location, 15, 27; as a factor in reinvestment, 29, 30, 36, 142; of outmovers, 106, 107, 108, 110; of those in survey, 68, 78, 81, 93. *See also* Households, female-headed; Households, single-person

Households, single-person, 170n.120; as a factor in displacement, 106, 111, 122; increases in number of, 17, 18; as participants in reinvestment, 18, 19, 26, 29; in survey, 78, 81, 86, 90, 93, 96, 122

Households, size of: changes in, 5, 12, 18, 19, 166n.26; control for, in survey, 108; as a factor in displacement, 106, 110, 111, 112–13; as a factor in housing needs, 105; as a factor in location, 15, 17, 19, 20, 26; as a factor in reinvestment, 30, 36, 37, 44, 72; of those in survey, 68, 76, 78, 81, 84, 90, 96, 108, 122–23

Households, transient, 66–67, 110, 119; in survey, 4, 67, 68, 69, 153–54

Housing: abandoned, 119, 140, 142, 170n.120; alternative, for displaced households, 7, 15, 42, 53, 54, 65, 115, 120, 122, 133, 135, 141, 163; changes in, as a factor in displacement, 103, 104, 105 (*see also* Condominiums,